2O/2O
LEADERSHIP

A 40-Year Career
in Hindsight

LEON DRENNAN

i

Additional books by Leon Drennan:

Empowering Progress
The Power of Purpose and Priorities – Leading the Way
People – Your Greatest Asset or Biggest Headache
Seasons of the Soul – Which one are you in?
Good King / Bad King – Which One Are You?

20/20 LEADERSHIP

A 40-Year Career
in Hindsight

LEON DRENNAN

Vision Leadership Foundation
Brentwood, TN

Published by Vision Leadership Foundation, Brentwood, TN 37027

ISBN 978-0-9978648-1-6

Scripture quoted in this book comes from one of the three sources noted below:

Scripture taken from the KING JAMES VERSION, public domain.

Scripture taken from the NEW AMERICAN STANDARD BIBLE®, Copyright © 1960, 1962, 1963, 1968, 1971, 1972, 1973, 1975, 1977, 1995 by The Lockman Foundation. Used by permission.

Scripture taken from THE HOLY BIBLE, NEW INTERNATIONAL VERSION®, NIV® Copyright © 1973, 1978, 1984, 2011 by Biblica, Inc.® Used by permission. All rights reserved worldwide.

The contents of this book are based on my recollection and understanding of Scripture as inspired by the Spirit and by a lifetime of leadership experience in a large, complex organization, as well as on the observation of others in leadership roles. My thoughts have been influenced by some great books and Christian authors as referenced in this book. Any perceived similarities to leadership or management materials in the marketplace are coincidental except those which I have specifically cited. — Leon Drennan, Vision Leadership Foundation

For more information about Vision Leadership Foundation, please visit:

www.Vision-Leadership.com
or, contact Leon Drennan at leon@vision-leadership.com

Dedication

I dedicate this book to my family. To Debbie, my wife of 42 years who has encouraged me in my writing and everything else of value that I've ever tried. To my children Scott, Allyson, and Kelsey. They gave me a reason to work long and hard and learn as much as I did in the process. Finally, I dedicate it to my grandchildren Francie Kate, Caden, Effy Joy, and Avery. They make me want to live longer and accomplish more with the life God gives me.

Acknowledgments

I appreciate the late Dr. Frist Sr., who modeled so well servant leadership at HCA, a for-profit corporation. I thank Dr. Frist Jr. for providing training and career opportunities for me beyond what I could have ever imagined. I thank the Frist family for modeling work/life balance and what family should look like.

I thank Diana Rush, who performed the executive support function for me through all of my books while working a fulltime job, managing a family, and caring for her aging mom.

Last, but certainly not least, I thank Fred MacKrell for guiding me through the process of writing and publishing all my books. If you are a first-time author, you need look no further than Fred to help you through the process.

Table of Contents

Preface

Experts say we get a sense of mission and purpose from something that makes us mad, glad, or sad. My motivation for writing this book and doing the other things I do stems from these three emotions for sure.

I coach, teach, and do strategic planning in the area of leadership. Why? Though I spent over 31 years in the healthcare business, I saw deeper and longer lasting pain on the faces of people who were being wounded by poor leadership than I did for clinical causes. It makes me angry that people could be in the business of healing and at the same time hurt others so deeply.

What I saw also made me sad. The company as a whole was such a good company and did such great things for people throughout the US and beyond. Yet so much more opportunity was wasted for leaders to lead effectively and create contentment and satisfaction in the lives of people.

To end on a positive note, my deepest gladness comes from helping people learn from the mistakes I made so they can be more effective leaders. I retired from the paycheck about 10 years ago and created Vision Leadership Foundation, a nonprofit organization. My goal is to invest my life in leaders to:

- Help them accomplish more in less time and with less stress. Leaders today seem to be running at a frenzied pace. They work hard and should be enjoying life. I want to help them have margin in their lives so there is more time for their spouses, children, churches, communities, friends, and overall enjoyment of life.

- Create a healthy culture wherever they are to benefit those they touch, especially employees. By applying the principles in this book, I believe leaders can empower employees to can get more done with less stress and greater contentment.

- Create more profit for business owners so they can share more financial resources with employees, ministries, and charities.

- Create better leadership and organizational administration for nonprofit organizations, ministries, and churches so that they are more effective in caring out their philanthropic missions.

I have a book called *Good King Bad King/Which One Are You?* So, why did I write this one? *Good King Bad King* is a 370-page leadership manual. It can be read like a book, but its best use is like a reference manual.

Also, over the past few years of coaching and teaching, I have learned some things that have sharpened and refined my thinking. The purpose of this book is to have something much shorter and in line with my current thinking. Using my theme "less is more," I'm trying to give you something that will be more impactful and take less of your time to read and absorb.

With over 40 years in organizational leadership at businesses, nonprofit organizations, ministries, and churches, I see a constant theme. Everybody wants that creative breakthrough idea that is going to sustain the organization as a success. Certainly, innovation and creativity are needed and allow organizations to provide more and better results over time. Yet many organizations fail, and most organizations tend to not live up to their potential because many basic principles are not followed consistently. This occurs even in innovative organizations. It's like watching professional sports teams lose important ballgames because very basic fundamentals were not followed. It's my strong contention that most sports games at that level <u>are not won</u> by superior talent but rather <u>lost</u> by the team that makes the most fundamental errors that day. I see some of the same challenges at work in organizations of all types. Therefore, I've looked back over my 40-year career of leadership in various roles to pick out those things that matter most in organizational life.

The idea behind this book is that I am using 20/20 hindsight to look back over a 40-year leadership career in business, churches, ministry, and nonprofits to see <u>what really mattered most.</u> Why does that matter? Because these same ageless, timeless basics will still matter the most in the next 40 years.

> Most competitions are not won by superior talent, whether it's sports or business. Most competitions are won by the team or organization that does the <u>basics</u> right consistently.

PURPOSE INTRODUCTION

The Cathedral

A man noticed three bricklayers who appeared to be doing exactly the same thing. He walked up to the first one and said, "May I ask what you are doing?" The man replied, "I am a bricklayer. I lay bricks on top of each other all day long and get paid $20 an hour to feed my family. It's hard work."

The gentleman asked the second man the same question. He replied, "I'm a builder. I love building. I get a good workout while I do my work. I don't have to work out early in the morning and then go do my job. And it lets me feed my family."

The gentleman went to the third man with the same question. The man replied, "Oh sir, I'm building a great cathedral. I love building. But this building is special. It will be grand and beautiful. Many people will gather here to admire its beauty. Their spiritual lives and destinies will be changed. I'm so lucky to have the opportunity to be part of this project. And can you believe it? I get to participate in something so special and actually be paid for it."

Everybody I know in business or any form of organizational life understands the importance of their people. I hear comments ranging from "business would be fun if it weren't for the people" to "I have the greatest team ever." Let's consider what makes organizational life either a pain or a joy, bricklaying or cathedral building.

The Perspectives

The three people are working on the same wall doing the same work. Yet they certainly have different perspectives. Why is that? There can be many reasons. Often, the bricklayer is operating outside their skill set or what I would call their sweet spot. Either they do not know or they are not rightly connected to the mission, vision, or priorities of the organization. There are many ways the leader or manager can impact a bricklayer's work. We will discuss some of those later.

The <u>builder</u> is using their skill set, operating within their sweet spot, but they are not necessarily passionate about the organization's mission/ vision. They may be able to see the vision of the completed project, but they focus primarily on their portion of the project. They take a certain pride in being part of it, but they may be willing to join any other project that uses their skill set appropriately.

The <u>cathedral builder</u> is committed to the mission, excited about the vision, has the talent to contribute, and feels lucky to be part of such a grand endeavor and still be paid.

As leaders, we need to wrestle with the fact that God didn't make anybody to just be a <u>bricklayer</u>. Each person is uniquely created for a specific purpose at a particular time in history that no one else can fulfill. Therefore, the question is, how do we move people from where they are to being cathedral builders? Obviously, we have to make sure we are meeting their most significant needs. What are they?

<u>The Bottom Line</u>

- The mission needs to be executed efficiently. Misalignment in the structural process to make progress causes inefficiencies, deviations from the mission, and frustration of the team.

- Leaders engage people. Managers use them.

- An organization of cathedral builders will be most effective and efficient.

Chapter 1

Leadership vs. Management

> **People need a sense of purpose, connection, and esteem.**

I've observed over many years that a set of basic and deep-seated needs must be met for a person to contribute their best to the organization.

Meaning: People have a deep need to matter, to be important, and make a difference in the world around them. Viktor Frankel made this clear many years ago in his book *The Meaning of Life*.[1] He wrote about how some people survived the Holocaust while so many didn't. Those who had a purpose or reason to continue to live beyond themselves tended to survive, while those who were focused primarily on themselves did not. Those who survived found some meaning in their pain. The meaning they found was in caring for and helping others in that horrible experience. In the context of work, people find meaning or significance in what they do and the organization they are part of. To be part of something bigger than ourselves. There is a limit to what we can

1

do or accomplish on our own. Since we all need to feel important, we like to be part of organizations that we take pride in and that make us feel more important than we would be on our own.

Vision: We all need vision or hope of a future that is better than today. It is part of how we are made. No matter what we have or what project we just finished, we tend to hope for more in the future. We are designed to make progress. We see this in the New Testament in the parable of the talents. Regardless of the talent level an individual had, God expected them to take it and multiply it. Hope of a better life in the future is engrained in all of us. Where there is no vision, there is no hope, and despair soon sets in. Scripture says, where there is no vision, the people perish. We may continue to breathe and exist, but there is no real life without vision. Only despair.

Social connection: We are social creatures. We were made for relationships with others and our Creator. The social connection at work is very important, since we spend most of our waking hours in the workplace. This is a key reason why the major firms that do employee surveys ask if you have a best friend at work. They know if that is the case, your likelihood of leaving for another job is greatly reduced.

Esteem: Everyone needs to feel valued and that they are esteemed. We want the respect of those around us—our coworkers and superiors. You may think that is the same as having meaning or being important. The fact is, we can be important and have meaning without being esteemed by our associates.

Security: We need to feel safe. We need to feel that our job is secure, that our work is acceptable, appreciated, and that our behavior is appropriate for the environment.

Progress: We need to make progress. Built within us is the desire for a future that is better than the present. We have to make progress to achieve that.

Leadership vs. Management

There is a big difference between leadership and management. Some managers may provide some leadership, and leaders do perform some management tasks. However, the best leaders manage through a leader's lens.

Managers:

- direct, and
- control people and tasks

They are more interested in a person's compliance than their passion and more interested in maintaining control than empowering people. That doesn't mean you can't have kind and benevolent managers, but they are still mostly focused on tasks and keeping control. By contrast, leaders:

- inspire with vision

- guide with priorities

- empower with goals

- encourage, coach, and correct for accountability

- share feedback and progress

The generation born in 1980 or later is called the Millennials. In fact, they are often called the "blank" Millennials. My generation, the Baby Boomers, and the generation after me, the Gen Xers, don't quite know what to do with Millennials. We are often confused and frustrated. It's important that we understand this generation population-wise is the largest in the world and soon will have the most purchasing power of any generation. Also, they are increasingly making up much of our workforce.

Dr. Kent Wessinger has done serious study and analysis of Millennials and has the best understanding of them that I've encountered. I do have some firsthand experience though, because I raised three of them.

3

One thing I am confident of is that Millennials will not be **managed**. But they will respond to good **leadership**. Why am I singling out this one generation? Because it is now the largest demographic in the world, will experience the largest transfer of wealth in history, and will make more than any previous generation. They will have a great influence on the world for the rest of my life.

It's possible to be in a manager's role and have a leader's mindset. It's also possible to be in a leader's role and have a manager's mindset. The difference is crucial, as we will begin to discover in Chapter 2 and beyond.

Chapter 2

The Highly Functional Organization

> **How much more could your organization accomplish if you would eliminate the dysfunction?**

For over 31 years, I worked in a large company with hundreds of sub-units, had dealings across the spectrum, and saw the functionality of hundreds of units. Since then, in my executive coaching and consulting role, I have seen how many organizations function. So the question is, in what type of organization can people's needs be met? Let's break this down in the following pages.

The following diagram depicts what I call the functional organization. We will describe each element of what makes an organization functional.

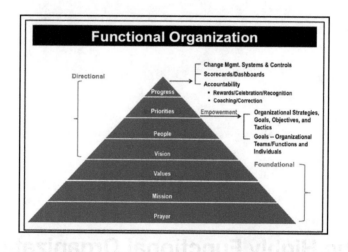

The foundation of an effective organization is prayer. Why? Because God knows the future and we don't. I don't care how visionary a man or woman is. They still don't know the future.

I know it's not politically correct to talk about prayer. Yet I can't properly explain any of the major success God granted in my life apart from prayer and God's action. If you're an organizational leader and not serious about your prayer life now, you may be during the next big recession. I know many business leaders got very serious in the last one.

As a practical matter, prayer settles the mind, emotions, and spirit. When we settle something in prayer, then we are less likely to make emotional and irrational changes to priorities later that distract the organization. I have seen people use three different approaches to prayer.

- "God, here is my plan, please bless it."

- When that doesn't work, then they pray, "God, here is my mess, please get me out of it."

- The best way to pray is, "God what is your plan and where do I fit into it?"

It is my prayer that God reveals the mission and vision of our organizations and our own lives as leaders.

Mission

The mission is why an organization exists and why stockholders fund it. If it is a nonprofit organization, the mission is why volunteers contribute their money and effort. A clear statement of the mission is important to keep an organization focused. It is the foundation upon which everything else is built. It matters because, as we said earlier, people need to be part of something bigger than themselves. The more they can identify with the mission, the more that need is met in their life. The more important they think the mission is, the more important they feel by being part of it. People want to work on things that matter. Leaders keep the mission in mind while managers focus on specific objectives. Millennials are even more likely to connect with a good mission than their predecessors.

Values

Values relate to how we work together. They are the accepted norms of behavior. Earlier, we said one of the basic needs of people is security. Values—how we work together, treat others, and treat our customers or constituents—help meet this need for security. There is a certain security in knowing your values and the organization's are in line. It's been proven many times in surveys that people will leave one organization for another for less money if there is greater alignment of values. Leaders establish and model the values. Managers comply with them.

When my daughter started college, she was going to get a degree in fashion merchandising. She found out in her first year the nature of the business is cutthroat competition. That's not her. It's not consistent with her personality or values. Because of that, she changed her major to pursue a career in line with her teamwork-oriented values. She has been very successful in it.

7

Vision

This is a picture of a better future. It can either draw a person to the organization or repel them from it. It tends to be inspirational, ignite a person's passions, and help draw a person to the organization. Scripture says that without vision, the people perish. That doesn't mean without vision we're going to immediately die. But without vision, a person's energy, inspiration, and passion die. Most importantly, hope dies. Despair is a slow form of death.

Leaders have a vision they want to share and have others join them as partners to achieve it. Managers, by contrast, have objectives they want others to help them achieve.

People

People tend to be attracted to or repelled by a vision. You want people attracted to your vision, not just a paycheck or a position. Attraction to a vision is what gives you a cathedral builder rather than a builder or a bricklayer. Here again, there is a striking difference between how a manager views people and how a leader views them.

Managers tend to look for competence and willingness. Is the person able to do this job? Are they willing to do it for this amount of money? After those questions are answered, managers typically make the offer.

Leaders tend to take a more holistic view in their assessment. They are looking for what I call the 5 P's in assembling their team:

Purpose — What were they created to do?

Personality — How were they wired and what are they good at doing?

Passion — What do they care deeply about?

8

Preparation — What is their training and experience?

Potential — What is their potential to grow in the role and in the organization?

The thought process of leaders and managers is very different. Managers tend to think, <u>how can I make them do what I want?</u> <u>The answer is, you don't!</u> That is the wrong question to ask.

Leaders are looking for alignment between the goals and aspirations of the individual and the vision of the organization.

Leaders empower people to do what they are good at, love doing, and want to do to help the organization achieve its mission and vision. They take a lot more time in the interview process to make sure there is alignment and the person fits the organization. They are concerned with the person being a good fit for the benefit of that individual as well as for the organization.

The ability to set and stick with priorities is vital to organizational effectiveness and progress. People want to work on something they believe is important. It helps them feel important. Even small kids have this need.

When my son was young, he always wanted to be with me doing yard work. When he was three and four years old, he wasn't really able to contribute to my work but he wanted to be with me and be involved. Sometimes I would send him to do a side project, but very shortly he would be back at my side wanting to do what I was doing. He intuitively knew what daddy was working on was what was really important. Some of the times he got most upset with me were when I was busy and didn't take time to let him feel like he was helping me with what I was doing. One time I was trying to plant a tree in the early spring and then water it. He wanted to help water. So I let him and next thing I knew, he was looking in the other direction and the water was running down my leg. It was pretty cold water that time of the year. Nevertheless, I knew he was going to insist on being involved and at my side.

Organizations that engage employees in establishing priorities get the best creative efforts of the team, as well as buy-in to the priorities. When employees are left out of the process and simply told what to do, that moves them in the direction of being bricklayers.

I worked for the same organization 31 years and considered myself to be a cathedral builder. However, there were seasons beyond my control when that wasn't the case. For a short portion of the time I led the Physician Services department, the environment was difficult and we were asked to hire physicians as quickly as we could. At other times, because of financial pressures, we were asked to terminate physician employment contracts. I'm not questioning the judgment or expertise of the executive leadership of the company. It was just a function of the times in a publicly traded company. However, when in one quarter you're hiring as fast as you can and the next you are terminating contracts, you are in essence putting bricks where you are told and then removing them when you're told. Sounds like a bricklayer function to me. At the same time, there were aspects of my role that were very strategic in building new initiatives, like the hospital-based physician initiative. Doing this, I was very much in cathedral-builder mode.

> **Where there are unclear or changing priorities, the organization forces people into a bricklayer mentality.**

Without a strategy or consistent set of goals, employees are left with having to respond to the next set of instructions.

One strength of a good leader is <u>setting</u> and <u>sticking with clear priorities</u>. In contrast, many managers often are not good at understanding priorities. They often have to be given priorities by the leader.

People were created for freedom and need freedom. They flourish in environments where they are free to do what they want to do, consistent with their hardwired skills and passions, to contribute to the organization. A question people often ask me is how to grant freedom but keep control. Part of the answer lies in the goal-setting process or <u>empowerment process</u>. Goals need to be set at the following levels:

- Total organization

- Operating subunits

- Corporate departments

- Teams

- Individuals

In essence, you start at the top and cascade goals through each level of the organization down to the individual. Each level of goals must support the next level. In other words, when you add up all the individual goals, they should accomplish the total organization's goals. Goals developed with the leader are cascaded to operating units, corporate departments, individual teams, and all the way to each individual.

This is an area where you see a real difference between executive leaders, managers, and micromanagers. Managers often like to hold things close to the vest and keep people on a short leash. They delegate tasks to people but keep a close watch. By contrast, leaders work with individuals to establish clear and mutually agreed upon goals that the individual is capable, willing, and even passionate about accomplishing. That's how you grant freedom.

Now, how do you keep control? We cover this in the Progress section, but the short answer is to establish proactive operational control and follow-up systems to ensure progress is being made while giving employees great freedom and latitude in pursuing their goals. I have found quarterly reviews to be a good tool to empower but maintain control. Each team member has clearly written goals with timeframes. Every quarter, they prepare a written update and review it with me. That way, the longest I can go without knowing their status and whether they are on track is 90 days. That gives them an opportunity to have an appropriate discussion when not under pressure and the leader a great chance to encourage and coach, if necessary.

When organizational goals are not achieved, the leadership should be able to go to the department that did not achieve its goals and all the way to the individuals who did not achieve theirs. When that occurs, often the thought is to terminate or discipline the individuals who did not meet their goals. That's how many managers look at it.

However, an effective leader should look at it this way. They should look at the next level up on the organizational chart to the person who delegated that work to the individual who didn't achieve their goals. It is the job of a leader and manager to give work to someone who is capable and willing to do it and then to support them in the process. If a goal is not met, the manager did not do a good job of delegating, or something may have happened beyond the control of the individual that kept them from meeting the goal.

I've heard so many business owners and managers talk about how bad their team is. They are constantly critical of their employees or volunteers. One of the worst cases I remember was a leader telling me he wished everybody on the team was as good at their job as he was at his. He used a football analogy and said he was ready to coach a team at the Super Bowl, but his team was just not ready. I thought to myself, as the leader, what does he think his job is? Either he hired the team or chose to keep them. He trained them. He empowered them. If the team was not up to speed, that meant he was not up to speed as a leader. It's amazing how many managers and people in leadership positions are so critical of their people, not realizing they actually are criticizing their own work.

People need to be part of an organization that makes progress and know how they contributed to it. At the end of a ballgame, the kids want to know two things: "Did we win?" and "How many points did I make?" In a sense, none of us really change from being a kid. We need to be on a winning team and we need to know how much we contributed. Think about it. We live in a country of sports fanatics. Would you really spend your time and money going to a ballgame where they didn't keep score? The answer for most people is absolutely not. So what is required for a team to make progress? Let's summarize and then discuss.

- Change
- Proactive change management systems that track progress
- Measurement with scorecards
- Feedback
- Coaching and accountability
- Celebration
- Correcting

Change

The first requirement to make progress is change. Doing the same thing you've always done and expecting a better result is the definition of insanity. The challenge is that some people don't like change. Good portions of the frontline people who do most of the work are hardwired to be skeptical of change. They still want to be on a winning team and to make progress though.

One job of an effective leader is to lead the change management process. Note that I said process. Just coming up with ideas and throwing them out to the group is not leading change. Effective change is a process that should be monitored through proactive controls to ensure steady and consistent progress without major setbacks.

Measurement

Progress should be measured through scorecards. Scorecards tend to be short-term oriented and track lead measures. Lead measures are those things that are controllable by individuals and teams that are predictive of the desired results. For example, a lead measure could be the number of calls made by a salesperson. Lag measures, by contrast, are usually tracked monthly, quarterly, or annually and report the actual results achieved. Feedback should be shared with employees regularly on how the team is doing and how they contributed.

Accountability

The final key to progress is accountability. Most people don't like this word because of the negative connotation it has received through mis-use or abuse by poor managers. Accountability is not negative at all when it includes the right components in the right order:

- Celebration, acknowledgment, and reward
- Coaching
- Correcting
- Discipline as a last resort

Celebration

When a person is in the right role at a healthy organization, doing what they are good at, have agreed to do, and love to do, <u>accountability should be about celebration, recognition, and awards</u>. Who wouldn't look forward to that? I tend to be a management by exception person. Reviewing performance quarterly helps me remember to do celebration regularly and to coach rather than criticize.

Why coach and correct?

Sometimes coaching and corrective actions are needed. If handled right, these can be constructive learning actions rather than a negative experience for the employee.

This stands in stark contrast to an environment where mistakes are pointed out in a critical, judgmental manner. Over time, people begin to feel like they can't do anything right. It is a depressing and low-performance culture. There are many people in management roles who will withhold positive feedback because they want to keep pressure on people for more.

One way managers fail to give employees their due is by not regularly giving them recognition, celebration, and reward (financial or non-financial) for their good work, or when they don't give them the information and security that they need to do their best. I see this in ministries some as well as businesses.

Coaching

Early in my career, I learned from Lee Iacocca's turnaround of Chrysler the importance of doing quarterly reviews, and I established that as a pattern. It ensured I did not go more than 90 days without recognizing and affirming the good work of my people. It also gave me an opportunity for a coaching time without micromanaging. I could make suggestions to people on how to improve their performance, which most people welcome if done properly.

If a person was off track with their goals, quarterly reviews ensured we did not go more than 90 days without my being aware of it and talking about ways to make course corrections. Team members tended to find security in the process. Most of the time, the quarterly review was a good experience for the individual and something they looked forward to. If it wasn't, the first thing I tried to figure out was what I had done wrong or could have done better to have avoided the situation.

The mentality of a coaching leader is very different then the mentality of a manager. Managers see their role as evaluating performance and providing objective feedback. They are quick to point out what was

15

done wrong. If the person isn't doing well, they start thinking about replacing them with someone else.

Coaches take leadership of the team and ownership of the final results. They believe in their team and see if there is a way to help them get better. Coaching comes across as a constructive learning experience while cold objective management feedback comes across as criticism. Millennials will respond well to coaching but very poorly to management.

Correcting

In rare instances, correction was needed. Again, we did not go more than 90 days without talking about the needed corrective action. Correcting is really coaching about how not to repeat mistakes.

Discipline

In very rare instances when necessary corrections were not made, then the disciplinary process began. If something unpleasant occurred, it did not happen at the end of the year and it was not a surprise to the individual. I always reserved discipline for repeated poor performance or one-time unacceptable behavior.

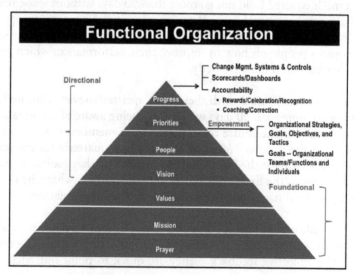

Summary

If you look at the functional organization pyramid as a whole, you will notice a few things.[2] One is that prayer, mission, and values are foundational. Build the organization upon these things. Without a firm foundation, the organization will crumble.

[2] *This source supports some of the ideas above in the triangle, but the original genesis is my experience.*

Notice also that from vision upward, all the elements are directional. That is, if you want to change the direction of an organization, you have to change the vision, attract the right people, establish the right priorities, and empower people to make progress toward that vision.

Finally, perfect alignment is illustrated by the straight red arrow. Every deviation represents inefficiency and ineffectiveness in achieving the mission. This causes extra work, frustration, and anxiety for the team.

Purpose Section Questions

1. Think about your staff, key leaders, and others. List your cathedral builders and your bricklayers.

2. What are your bricklayers costing you?

3. How will you help your bricklayers become cathedral builders?

4. How do you make your mission and vision real to the average person?

Chapter 3

The Dysfunctional Organization

> How much happier and more
> productive would your team be if
> you eliminated the dysfunction?

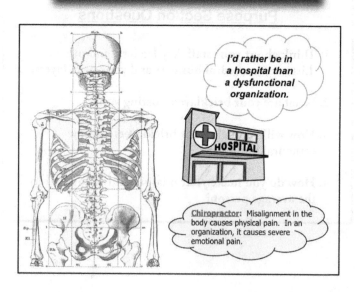

I've often said I would rather be in the hospital than in a dysfunctional organization. Look at the slide above. The skeleton reminds me of diagrams you see in chiropractors' offices. I've had my share of back issues and, therefore, have an appreciation for these diagrams. Anytime the back has misalignment, it results in serious physical pain until the misalignment is adjusted.

In organizational life, great pain is created through misalignment. However, the pain is not physical pain. It's mental and emotional. Misalignment in organizations increases the <u>stress</u>, <u>frustration</u>, <u>anxiety</u>, and <u>fear</u> of the employees. Over my career, I counseled a great number of employees in my office literally in tears because of the emotional pain caused by dysfunction in some other part of the organization. The pain is real and it continues. Among the teenage culture, there's an issue called "cutting" where adolescents are in such an emotional pain that they cut themselves to create a physical pain that distracts from the emotional pain.

So, why would I rather be in the hospital than in a dysfunctional organization? In a hospital:

- I expect to get better
- There is pain medicine even before I'm healed that gives me relief from the pain
- If I don't get better, I'm going to die and go to heaven. The pain ends.

In the dysfunctional organization, there is no hope of getting better and no good pain relief unless you turn to drugs or alcohol. These are temporary and exacerbate the problem. Despair and hopelessness set in as the pain continues.

The next diagram is a picture of a dysfunctional organization. Nothing aligns.

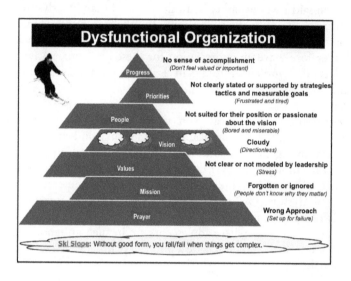

In this organization, **prayer** is not foundational. Therefore, when hard times come, the mind, body, and spirit are not aligned and many changes made are not productive.

The **mission** is forgotten or ignored. Therefore, people don't know why their work is important. Also, mission creep is often experienced, which diffuses the focus of the organization.

The **values** are not clear or not modeled by the leadership. Employees experience stress because they don't know what behavior is acceptable and don't feel the security of values they agree with.

The **vision** is cloudy. People feel their organization is directionless. This causes hopelessness and despair rather than energy and passion.

People are not suited for their positions or are not passionate about what they do. They get bored and miserable.

Priorities are not clearly stated and supported by strategy, tactics, and goals or they are constantly changing. Employees get frustrated and tired. They see much of what they're doing as meaningless or wasted effort.

The organization is not making **progress**. Employees have no sense of accomplishment and don't feel important.

You may be in a small organization and feel like you're keeping everything on track. However, your current experience may compare to my snow skiing abilities. On an easy slope, I look like I know what I'm doing. When you put me in deeper snow or on a more difficult slope, you quickly see that I do not have the form or the experience to stay on my feet. I typically tumble end over end. As your organization grows and gets more complex, the management methodologies you employed when it was smaller typically won't work anymore and you're heading for a fall.

PRIORITIES
INTRODUCTION

I once did a consulting project with a nonprofit organization. It did very good work but was not in good shape administratively. The staff was overwhelmed and frantically running itself in circles. To help them, I called a team meeting to agree upon some priorities. To take pressure off the other team members, I asked the chief administrative leader to state his priorities first. He stood in front of the group with a sheet of yellow legal paper. It was filled front and back with what he called his priority list. I quickly determined we didn't have time that afternoon to both go over his list and even get started with the rest of the group. I asked him to share his top three priorities. He got this strange, confused look. He lifted both hands, palms up, shook his head and said, "I have no idea." Here's the issue. If he's the chief administrative leader and has no idea about his priorities, how can he expect anybody else to be clear about theirs?

This was a good ministry that did good work. It had good and well-intentioned people. Everyone was doing their best. But without clear priorities, the culture was characterized by anxiety, chaos, confusion, and fear.

The previous section, Purpose, is especially critical. If you don't understand the purpose of your organization and your purpose for being there, you will not be able to set and maintain meaningful priorities. Your understanding and commitment to a purpose will give you the endurance to overcome obstacles and persevere personally and organizationally toward significant accomplishments.

Everywhere I go, I see people in a hurry and frustrated. The best word I can use to describe them is frenzied. And the problem is getting worse. Why is this occurring? There are two important reasons. One is they don't know why they do what they do. They don't understand their purpose. The other is that they don't have a sense of focus or priorities. They treat too many things as of equal importance. They are trying to do too much. They are not accomplishing all they would like to. Their energy is drained. Their frustration builds. They intuitively know something is wrong but don't know how to fix it. Less than 5 percent of the people I know have a clue about their purpose or mission in life. It's not something most people think about deeply. And they suffer the consequences of not answering this all-important question.

The solutions to a lack of priorities are easy to articulate, but hard for most people to implement. How do you set clear, consistent, and meaningful priorities if you're not clear about your purpose in life? Equally important is that if you're not clear about your purpose, you will not have the endurance to overcome obstacles and persevere to significant accomplishments.

Priorities separate the really important from the rest of your activities. When priorities are completed, you have a sense of accomplishment because you know something that really mattered got done. When you know what God put you on this earth to do, then you can discern what your priorities need to be. Otherwise, you tend to chase the urgent, do what's easy first, or simply please the people around you.

Purpose not only helps clarify priorities, but it helps us accomplish our priorities. Usually, important things take longer and are harder to accomplish than the other things on our daily schedule or to-do list. When you're trying to accomplish important and difficult things with your life, you need stamina and endurance. What gives you endurance?

23

The Bottom Line

- Unclear priorities, changing priorities, or too many priorities will result in confusion of the team, diffusion of the effort, and disillusionment of the team.

- Leaders execute based on priorities while managers execute based on projects.

Chapter 4

PRIORITIES

> **If you are a leader and don't know your priorities, how can you expect the rest of the team to know theirs?**

Why don't leaders know their priorities? There are several reasons or combinations of reasons why the situation described in the section introduction occurred:

- The leader was a very competent person able to do many things, and work naturally flowed to him.

- He had a people-pleasing personality and seldom said no to anyone.

- He was highly respected by his boss who delegated many things to him that did not go with his job description. In fact, this evolved until the guy was doing the job of two people. It became too much and his boss was not happy, nor was he.

- He let his team delegate up to him.

25

- He was very good at doing work, but not at all good at prioritizing it.

So what can you do about a situation like this? We will talk about that a bit later.

Let's look at priorities through this lens: Suppose I went to the bank and got a lot of cash and laid it on the table before you as depicted in the following diagram.

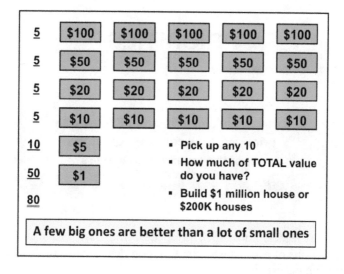

You see five $100 bills, five $50s, five $20s, five $10s, a stack of 10 $5s, and a stack of 50 $1s for a total of 80 different bills totaling $1,000. If I said you could have any 10 bills you wanted, which 10 would you pick up?

Most people would select the five $100 bills and five $50 bills. That totals $750 or 75 percent of the $1,000 lying on the table. Yet the person is only picking up 10 out of 80 total bills available. It takes the same effort approximately to pick up $750 worth of bills as it does to pick up 10 $1 bills.

You may say, "True, but it takes more time to earn $100 than it does to earn $1." That's not always true unless you are an hourly wage earner. What if you are a builder? You might build a $200,000 house for a 20% fee and earn $40,000. In building a house, you line up subcontractors and inspect their work. What if you arrange to build a $1 million house for a fee of 10%? Your total compensation would be $100,000. That's 2 1/2 times the $40,000 for the $200,000 house. However, you invest nowhere near 2 1/2 times as much effort and time in that project. When you order the brick and inspect it, there's not much difference in the time for the small house versus the big house.

In organizational life, you have high-impact projects and lower-impact projects. Certain aspects of those projects take the same amount of time regardless of the project's importance. For example, take team meetings. Meetings usually take about the same amount of time whether it's a high- or low-priority project.

The obvious conclusion is that you get more done in an organization if you have a few high-impact projects rather than a bunch of low-priority projects.

Nature Speaks

Picture a river in your mind's eye. The river is two miles wide and has barges, boats, and dinghies on it. They are spaced a safe distance apart with each carrying cargo. A certain amount of goods can be moved in a day's time on this river, even without any other power source, because it is flowing five miles per hour. If you wanted to move the most goods down the river in the least amount of time, what would you do?

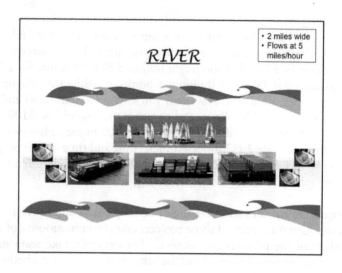

Let's assume you had the ability to narrow the banks of the river. Now, instead of being two miles wide, it's a mile wide and flowing at ten miles per hour. For this to be safe, you have to take the sailboats and dinghies off the river and all you have left are the barges. In this scenario, would you be able to move more goods in less time? Of course you would.

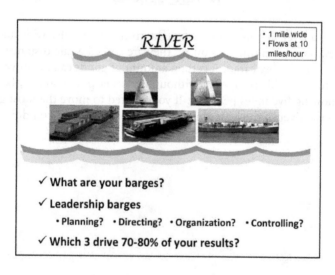

28

Now, let's think about any area of your life and see if an analogous principle holds true. Take work for an example. Let's compare the width of the river to the breadth of the project lists and activities you have. As leaders, we have many choices to narrow the number of activities we engage in and the number of projects we pursue. Now let's compare the barges to those projects and activities that really "move the needle." As leadership used to say at HCA: "Big things have the greatest impact." Let's compare the sailboats in organizational life to those projects or initiatives that have particular individuals' thumbprints on them. They are matters of pride, flashy and fast compared to barges. These are smaller projects that can move quickly, but over time they don't do much to "move the needle." The only sailboat-type projects that should be left in place are those that have the potential for barge-type impact later. Now let's compare the dinghies in organizational life to pet projects of the leader. These are small blips on the radar screen and the leader can control them, but they do nothing to "move the needle." These projects still take administrative time and effort, and they take some resources. Dinghy-type projects should be eliminated.

When the focus is narrowed to the big projects that really "move the needle," more progress is made in a shorter period of time. We see this in the Bible in the book of Nehemiah. The great wall of Jerusalem was rebuilt in 56 days, a task thought unachievable. How did this happen? It was the single focus of all the people, and they did more than they thought possible during that timeframe.

Most books on time management have a number of tricks and techniques that are useful in helping you be more efficient with your time. But I know through experience that narrowing my focus and concentrating on the high-potential projects always yields the best results.

> **The key to time management is priority management.**

Chapter 5

What Moves The Needle For Leaders?

Do you know the three key activities that "move the needle" for leaders?

During my early years in the Audit Department, I functioned like a manager or micromanager, certainly not a leader. I felt a need to know everything, seldom took vacation, and it was hard for me to be away for long. I felt like I needed to be there every day to know what was going on, with the illusion that I was in control.

As I made the transition from manager to leader, I learned there was a better way. I worked with the team to create plans, empowered the team with clear goals, and implemented an enabling control system. I actually knew more about what was going on and the status of the functions I led than before, when I always needed my hands on them. Learning this in the audit function helped me immensely when I led Physician Services. The practices we managed and the team I led spread across 20 states. There was no way I could micromanage that.

30

So, what are the things that "move the needle" for a leader? This will depend on the nature of your organization and its size and scale. I will share the "needle movers" in my last organizational role. Leading the team in <u>planning</u> to come up with clear priorities and breaking those into strategies and goals by department and individual took about <u>5-10%</u> of my time each year. This was one of the most critical activities I did each year because it directed everyone's focus.

Putting the right <u>people</u> in the right place took another <u>5-10%</u> of the time. From years of experience, I can tell you that having the right people in place is the difference between a good life for leaders and misery for them and the team. As important as it is to get the right people in place, I observed frequently that otherwise good leaders would get really busy and not put the necessary time and focus into interviewing and filling positions with the right people. There were times in turnaround situations when I had to make leaders give priority to people selection. They kept "putting out fires," not realizing there was no end to it until they got the right people in place and delegated to them appropriately.

<u>Accountability</u> took about <u>10-15%</u> of my time. Setting up good control systems with exception reporting and variance monitoring can take more time early on. However, once such systems are established, determining whether you are within the boundaries and what needs to be done if you are not takes only a small portion of your time.

This is the approach I used at HCA to expand Physician Services and the company's temporary nurse staffing organization at the same time I served in the role of executive pastor at my church. For each area, we made sure we had good plans that everyone understood and to which everyone was rightly connected. We put the right organization chart in place and put the right people in the proper positions. Then we implemented measurement and control systems to monitor if we were proceeding according to plan. I delegated much to capable leaders. Following this approach allowed me to do many different things without running out of time. We made progress in all of those areas. Sounds easy, doesn't it? Now, what are the mistakes leaders make regarding priority management?

Three Things That Kill Progress

Unclear priorities

I remember trying to assess priorities of a new corporate department for which I had assumed responsibility. It quickly became clear there was no true sense of priorities. Those in the department were simply trying to make operators happy. Naturally, there was much wasted activity. Substantial money was being spent on plans and projects that had no hope of being approved. There was much other wasted activity with no sense of direction. Some of the activity even worked against the company in the long run.

I led the team to assess strengths, weaknesses, opportunities, and future threats. From that analysis, we put together a set of goals and priorities and had them endorsed by senior management. The team saved millions of dollars and did a better job for the company with much less stress and anxiety because they had clear priorities.

Too many priorities

One of my group vice presidents came back from a division presidents meeting one time and was quite excited about the priorities the division president presented. I looked at his sheet of notes and quickly said, "Problem." He looked at me astonished and asked what was wrong with the priorities. He asked me which ones I didn't like. I said, "Each of them is fine. The problem is there are 13 of them. Can people focus clearly on 13 different things?" My experience is if you go beyond five to seven objectives/priorities for an annual cycle, you start diluting the effort, and people lose focus.

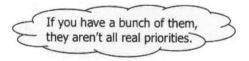

If you have a bunch of them, they aren't all real priorities.

So how does focusing on priorities in your organization help people? It brings simplicity to complexity. It ensures people are pulling together toward the key priorities, resulting in greater accomplishment and satisfaction for them and the whole team. It assures the leader and employees are on the same page, resulting in fewer expectation gaps, conflicts, and instances of confusion.

Let's think about how a river works. The more the river banks narrow, the deeper the channel gets and the faster and stronger the water flows. Priorities in organizations act like river banks. Narrowing them makes initiatives flow faster and stronger. Priorities create "tipping points" in organizations like the great waterfall on a river. Things move with great speed, and a powerful, almost unstoppable force is created. It has great power and beauty.

Constantly Changing Priorities

When leaders constantly change directions, it may look like the diagram below. Everything to the left and right of the dotted line represents wasted time, energy, and resources. The people working on a project like this see it clearly. In an organization with constant changes, the team is bewildered by the amount of waste they see.

Constant priority changes cost the organization in three important ways:

Opportunity cost. The opportunity cost in this scenario is significant. The time, energy, and resources spent going the wrong direction could have been spent on something of real value. This creates great frustration for the team.

Lost initiative. When priorities constantly change, individuals cease to be proactive and think ahead. They simply wait for the next change to be announced by the manager. When people quit taking initiative, you've lost their best forward thinking and their best creativity. If this happens to a sizable team of people, the opportunity cost to the organization is extraordinary. Yet it happens frequently.

Turnover. In this kind of environment, the team gets increasingly frustrated. The best and most capable team members will use their desire to be proactive by seeking and finding other jobs. That leaves you with the lower performing team members while your competitors now have your higher performers. Over time, this can dramatically change the competitive landscape within an industry.

Chapter 6

Pruning and Focus

You have to focus on doing fewer projects to produce better results.

I've heard thousands of sermons over my lifetime. A handful of them really stand out in my mind. One was a sermon by Dr. George Horton. His primary theme was:

Not many things matter in life, but what matters, matters mighty much.

This reminds me of the movie *City Slickers*, where a guy from the city was told by an old cowboy that only one thing matters in life. The city guy asked, "What?" and the cowboy said, "That is what you have to figure out."

As you go through life, you're given many opportunities to do many things. Most people try to do too many, and that's why they seem to be anxious and worn out a lot of the time. They have to make choices they don't want to make.

Hourglass

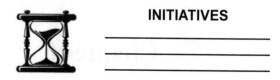

INITIATIVES

Everybody has a set amount of time. It's like the hourglass is running. So you have to choose what you will focus on. You can do a lot of low-priority initiatives or many fewer higher-priority initiatives. Most people try to do too many things with the time they have available. They call them all priorities, but only a few truly are or should be. The overabundance of supposed "priorities" can cause projects to be mediocre or fail outright. This is particularly damaging when it's a high-priority project that fails.

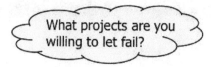

What projects are you willing to let fail?

The alternative is to limit the number of activities and initiatives. Then put all your time on high-priority projects that will give you the best result.

Now let's go back to the nonprofit administrative leader with whom we begin this section. How do we fix his dilemma? For anybody in a large organization, a certain amount, and often a large amount, of time is spent on required administrative meetings, reports, and other interactions. So you only have a limited amount of marginal time available. The key is to be very clear about setting priorities and focus that limited time on things that are going to produce the best results. It's better not to try to do this alone, but rather engage the broader team and make sure all the personality types are represented so you are truly setting good priorities for the team and the organization.

<u>Pruning</u>

To me, less is more in all areas of life. I don't think you can make your life better just by being busier in any area. I grew up on a farm, so I tend to think we can learn a lot from nature. One counterintuitive thing nature teaches us is that having the healthiest and most robust plants requires pruning. Yes, you have to cut things back—prune them—so they may reach their optimal health, growth, and beauty. Dr. Henry Cloud, in his book *Necessary Endings*, teaches us this through his illustration of pruning rose bushes.[3]

 Three kinds of branches need pruning on a rosebush:

- **Dead branches that are taking up space needed for healthy ones.** Evaluate all areas of your life. What activities are dead—those that bring you no joy, give you no feeling of purpose, and are not necessarily helping anyone else? You do these out of habit or obligation. Cut these out.

- **Sick branches that aren't going to get well.** These are activities in any area of your life that have some life. They aren't totally useless, but they don't bring real joy or meaning, and that's not going to change. Cut these out.

- **Healthy branches that aren't the best.** My pastor, Mike Glenn, always says "good is the enemy of best." There are activities in your life that are good. They bring you joy, help other people, and you see purpose in them. Yet they take time that could be spent on even more purposeful activities with more impact for you and others. Cut them out to allow time for the best.

It is sometimes surprising to see what people will give up in life to achieve a particular goal or complete a project at their job. Often people make significant tradeoffs for projects they won't remember a year later. I remember many times almost insisting that employees take time off to be with sick parents or to be at some significant event for their children.

I'm convinced they would not have done it without my encouragement. I was impressed by their dedication but marveled at their lack of insight regarding the true priorities in life. I say that remembering some poor decisions I made myself, especially early in my career. I wish I could go back to make more holistic and conscientious decisions about what matters most in life.

Focus

People, especially leaders, are the busiest I have ever seen them. Leaders want more time, more freedom, and less stress. How is that even possible in organizational life today? The key is how you approach life. Are you going through life like a rifle bullet or like a shotgun blast? Let me explain. A rifle bullet is much smaller than the shotgun shell. It has less powder and less lead. It takes less powder because there's only one piece of small lead at the end as it leaves the barrel moving straight toward its target. It takes less powder to propel the smaller piece of lead a great distance. By contrast, a shotgun shell has much more powder and more lead. The lead is a bunch of pellets, called buckshot. They look like small BB's. They come out of the shotgun barrel and scatter, hitting a bigger target area. The shooter can be less accurate with a shotgun and still hit the target. But since the buckshot scatters and is small, it doesn't go nearly as far as a rifle bullet.

Both types of ammunition are like some people's lives. Some people are highly focused on a singular objective or a limited number of objectives, and they can go far. Other people's lives have so many activities that they are more like a shotgun blast. They cover a lot of territory but don't make as much progress as the person who is more focused.

Balance

While establishing clear priorities in our lives is important, it's also important that we have balance. Jesus was a great example of how to live a balanced life. You are likely familiar with the Ralston Purina checkerboard square illustrated on the next page. I'm told the founder established this as the symbol for his company based upon Luke 2:52.

"And Jesus increased in wisdom and stature

and in favor with God and man."

Luke 2:52

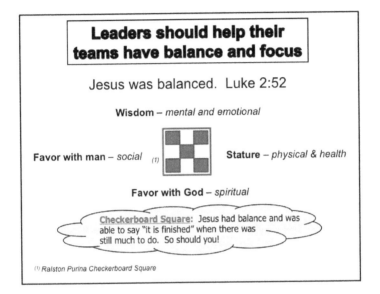

One thing I notice about Jesus is that he was never in a hurry. Not one time. Yet, he grew mentally, emotionally, physically, in good health, spiritually, and socially. His earthly ministry only lasted three years. There were still people to be preached to, converted, healed, and ministered to in a variety of ways. Yet Jesus was content ending his day after he did all Father told him to do. He went to extended wedding feasts that lasted days and to dinners that lasted all evening. Yet he didn't seem stressed that he had not done something he was supposed to do that day.

At the end, Jesus said from the cross, "It is finished." Yet there was so much more work to be done to reach the world. His message was simple. He had accomplished his mission or purpose and done all he came to do. How many days in a week can you go home and leave work behind, knowing it's finished, that you accomplished all you were supposed to for that day? If you can't do that, then likely your life is out of balance.

Who's in control?

If I can influence two key things in an organization's life, then I can influence its direction and what it accomplishes. Those two things are priorities and the control system. Priorities determine direction and focus. If I can influence those, I can change the direction of the organization to some degree. I don't have to be with people every day, live in the same city, state, or even country as long as I can influence the priorities. I also need to be able to influence the control system because that is what determines how well the priorities get executed.

Priorities Section Questions

1. Do you know what is most important in your organization?

2. Do your employees?

3. Do you have only a few key priorities?

4. Are you consistent with priorities or do you change them frequently?

POWER – PART I
INTRODUCTION

KEEP IT OR SHARE IT?

I was raised on a small farm, for which I'm grateful. We had dairy cows, but also raised hogs to sell. The hogs were a problem. They tended to get outside the fence and root the grass in our fields. So Daddy bought and installed an electric fence. He would test to see if the electric fence was working by taking a shovel, sticking it in the ground, and leaning the metal part against the fence. When it was working, it would create a small spark.

Sometimes, when we fed the hogs, some grains of corn would fall close to or under the electric fence. The hogs would touch the fence, get shocked, squeal, and jump back. As a kid, I thought that was funny. Sometimes, I would drop kernels of corn leading up to the fence, knowing the hogs would focus on the corn and touch the fence. It worked 100% of the time. They always went after the corn and hit the fence. I wasn't doing it to be mean. I just thought it was funny.

Then, I decided to escalate the game. I tied a string to an ear of corn. The hogs would go for it, and I would pull the corn toward the fence. In going for the corn, two or three hogs would touch the fence, squeal, and jump back. They weren't really hurt. Just a little shocked. I felt smart, in control, and it seemed funny to me.

I got creative and decided to escalate the game again. I climbed up the fence and climbed from the top of the fencepost to the top of a small shed which was about nine feet high. I tied an ear of corn to a string and lowered it to the ground. The hogs would go for it, and I would pull it just out of their reach. They would chase it, and I would continually pull it just out of their reach. That was entertaining for a while. Then, I decided I wanted to see if I could make them dance. So when they were fully engaged in going for that piece of corn, I lifted it just above their heads. They would stand on their hind legs snapping at the ear of corn. I had made them dance!

Sometimes, they would get the ear of corn in their mouth, and I would jerk it out. A couple of times, they got a good hold on the corn and were able to jerk the string out of my hand. The string burned my hand. Plus, I had to climb off the roof to get the string again.

When I had enough of that, I wrapped the string around my hand so they wouldn't be able to jerk it out as easily. What happened next was rather predictable. I was confident they couldn't jerk the string from my hand, so I took a little more risk. I let them get the corn in their mouth and then jerked it out. There was one 500-pound hog that was standing straight up on her hind legs. She got the ear of corn locked firmly in the back part of her jaw. She flicked her big strong neck, and I came sailing off the roof like a missile.

It had been a while since the last rain. So the once-muddy hog lot was dry and hard with lumpy clumps of dirt. As the hog dragged me across those rock-hard clumps, my chest and groin area were catching the brunt of the punishment. Thank God, after a few yards, the string broke. The hog had the corn, and I was free.

At the point in this story where I said I wanted to make the pigs dance, was your first thought, "I wonder how he's going to make a pig dance?"

Or was your first thought, "Why would you want to make a pig dance?" You see, why I wanted to make a pig dance showed a lot about my motives. I wanted power and control. I wanted to be entertained at the pig's expense. That was wrong, and it was costly.

As you can see, I desired the wrong kind of power. But I learned a valuable lesson. I tend to think abuse of power starts very early in life with others too. We either grow beyond it or stay trapped in it.

> Why would you want to make a pig dance?
> Why do you enjoy manipulating people?

The Bottom Line

- Growth of the organization is substantially limited unless people are properly empowered.

- People who are micromanaged do not offer initiative or creativity to the organization.

- Leaders empower people while managers control people.

Chapter 7

What Is Power?

Do you understand how to use power to make work easier for yourself and others?

Now that we have discussed abuse of power, let's talk about what power is and how to use it positively. The most common answer I get when I ask people to define power is, in a nutshell, <u>influence</u>.

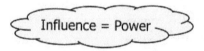

Influence = Power

There is a biblical view of power and a worldly view. Over the past few years, as I've had the opportunity to travel in Europe and to learn its history, I have gotten a better sense of the world's view of power. Basically, it comes down to control. Kings and monarchs of past years had absolute authority over people and every aspect of their lives. Most kings sought to keep absolute control over their people more than anything else. That's why Jesus' leadership was so radical in his day. He did not try to control people. His goal was not to be served.

He introduced to the world servant leadership by saying, "I came not to be served, but to serve and give my life for many." Servant leadership does exist in varying degrees in some organizations, but it remains a struggle for many. Very broadly, I see three types of power that people use.

Personal power. This is influence related strictly to the individual without regard to their position in an organization. The good thing about personal power is that it goes with you wherever you go. If you have acted with integrity, treated people well, and helped people along the way, they tend to listen to you and do what you suggest. If you have been serving people well, over time they tend to listen to you, and what you say has a great deal of influence over their decision making and, therefore, their lives.

Let me tell you a story about Dr. Frist, Sr.—one of the three founders of HCA. My aunt had been diagnosed with pancreatic cancer. She was in horrible pain and wanted a second opinion from a physician in Nashville. The family asked me who was best. At that time, I was a young executive and had no idea who she should see. I asked for an appointment with Dr. Frist, Sr. My only goal was to ask him for the name or names of the best physicians for her to see.

 He said, "wait a minute" and quickly turned around and got a physician on the phone. He said, "I have someone I want you to see when are you available." It was Friday, and the physician apparently said Tuesday of the next week. Dr. Frist, Sr. met my aunt and family in the physician's lobby. He talked to them before and after they saw the doctor. Dr. Frist, Jr. also ran the company as a results-oriented executive while showing great compassion in his leadership style.

That's the kind of company I grew up in. Our founders were servant leaders. They had a heart and compassion for people. Work was never a game for them, and they took every day seriously. They didn't play games with people's lives. They made people's lives better. The remarkable thing about my story of Dr. Frist, Sr. is that it is one of hundreds that could be told about the man. I shared this one because it was my own experience. Dr. Frist had tremendous personal power until the day he died. This is why!

Positional Power. Positional power, also called "legitimate power," is the power of an individual because of his or her position and duties within the organization.[4] It is the kind of power that can say, "Because I said so and I'm the boss." Usually it is not said that directly, but inferred by what is said or by the tone of voice and body language. People are respecting or acquiescing to the authority of the position, but not necessarily the person unless they happen to respect them. Positional power stays with the position but not necessarily the individual, unless they also have personal power. I have known individuals who did not use their positions well and once they were no longer in them, some people with whom they thought they had a relationship wouldn't even return their calls.

Organizational Power. This is power the organization has to influence people. Look back at the pyramid image at the very beginning of the book, and let's think about how organizations influence people's behavior. People are influenced by, among other things, the mission, values, vision, and priorities of the organization.

Servant Leadership

Now is a good time to ask if you are or want to be a servant leader. To be a servant leader, you have to have the right kind of heart.

A relatively young man was washing his bright red sports car at the public car wash, and he attracted the attention of a 9-year-old boy. The young lad peppered him with questions and comments such as, "Mister, you must work a lot of hours to own a car like that!" to which the young man replied, "No, I don't work a lot of hours." The boy said,

46

"Then you must have a really high-paying job to own a car like that." The young man replied, "No, son, I don't have a high-paying job."

The boy scratched his head, thought, and said, "Well then, you must own the company to be able to own a car like that," to which the young man replied, "No, son, I don't own the company."

To avoid further questioning he said, "Look, son, I don't work a lot of hours, I don't make a lot of money, I don't have a big job, and, in fact, I don't even have a job. The truth is my big brother bought me this car."

The little boy looked down and kind of pawed at the ground with his foot. He stuttered and said, "Mister, I wish, I wish, I wish." The young man, sure he knew what the young boy would say, was going to go ahead and finish the thought for him. Something along the lines of "I know. You wish you had a big brother like that." Before he got it out, the boy finished his sentence and said, "Gee, mister, I would sure like to be a big brother like that." The young man was stunned and carried that response with him the rest of his life.

I hope you carry this thought with you as well. If you don't truly have in your heart the desire to be like that big brother, to do something extraordinary for somebody else, please get out of the business of trying to be a leader.

The question is, do you have a heart to serve and help other people? If you don't, the world would be a better place if you got out of management. If you do, you might make a good manager and an excellent leader.

> The only people who should be trusted with power are servant-minded leaders.

47

Chapter 8

Using Power Correctly

> How much more would you enjoy your work
> if people did what you asked eagerly and
> without grumbling or complaining?

I have noticed a tendency for small businesses to hit barriers and stay small. Nonprofit organizations spring up everywhere, but only a few get large. There are megachurches in the United States, but most churches are small, under 100 people. Why is that? Why do so many businesses, churches, and other organizations tend to plateau and seem unable to grow any further? The key is how they approach the use of power. Are they going to approach it as Moses did when he started out? He kept all the power, and people gathered around him waiting for him to judge their cases and give them direction. Or are they going to approach power the way Jethro suggested to Moses? That way was to identify capable leaders, provide training, and empower them to act on most cases, keeping only the hardest cases for the chief executive.

Why Small Organizations Stay Small and Large Organizations Get Bigger

Today, we might refer to these approaches as the "mom and pop" or sole proprietor model and the franchise model. Growing up in a small town, I observed the sole proprietor approach at the local grocery and hardware stores. They had few employees, and everything revolved around the owner. HCA gave me the opportunity to experience a different style of leadership, one common in large companies and franchises. In the first instance, the power is retained by the owner or the founder. In the second, power is distributed to a number of other people.

Mom and Pop Organizations

Small businesses and organizations often stay small because the focus is on the owners/founders. They always have control. We see this model throughout society. In some local businesses, the owners are always there making the decisions. When they're out, the employees have to call or wait for them to return before making a decision outside the norm.

When organizations are led like this, they never grow larger than what the individual leaders can touch. What's the difference between a person owning and running one restaurant and the same person owning and running 10, 20, 30, or even 100 restaurants? With some basic skills in the restaurant business, people can run a single restaurant. However, to run 10 restaurants or 100, they have to approach the business much differently, like a franchise. What makes franchises and large organizations like HCA different?

- Operating manuals for each key aspect of the organization indicating how things are to be done

- Measurement of certain key activities and standards for what is expected

- Checks and balances so that activities have an acceptable level of control but are not stifled

49

- Information technology and management reporting, so leaders can know what's going on without always being there physically to observe. Franchises require goals for individual business units and goals, coupled with good training, for each position in the organization. They have great policy and procedure guides, operating manuals, training systems, and control systems. Managers are carefully selected and trained to operate successfully within acceptable boundaries.

In franchise systems, the owners/leaders can't be in every restaurant every day. But when the operating parameters are properly established, levels of service quality and profitability can be consistently achieved. With good management reporting systems and controls, the owners can know where each restaurant stands in a timely manner.

What do large organizations do that small organizations don't? Generally, they are more sophisticated in using documentation, training, policies, and procedures to guide the organization. Small organizations tend not to have developed and refined operating manuals, written policies and procedures, control systems, and management reporting systems. They tend to accomplish things by the owners'/founders' individual engagement and oversight. Therefore, they can't grow beyond what the leaders can be engaged in.

Using Power

If you are an owner or manager, you must choose how to use power. Very broadly, there are two approaches: keep it or share it. I've always been fascinated by Old Testament characters and have learned a lot about leadership and management from their approaches. First, I look at Moses in his early days. I see in my mind's eye a long line of people coming to get their complaints heard and receive further directions from Moses. He had a great heart and dearly loved the people. He was a great spiritual man and completely morally and ethically clean. But when it came to power, <u>Moses was an autocrat in his early days</u>.

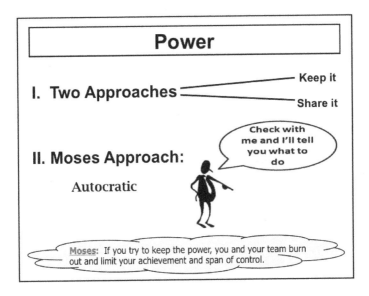

Moses started his career micromanaging. Besides manipulating, like I had tried to do with the pigs, another form of mismanagement is trying to control people through micromanaging. By natural hardwiring, as well as how I was raised, I fight this issue also.

So what is micromanaging? It's basically looking over people's shoulders and trying to control every detail of what is going on. This usually happens in small businesses or small nonprofits. That is one reason they stay small. Micromanaging can be done to a certain level of success, but only when an organization stays small.

An organization cannot grow safely or successfully under this kind of management. The results over time can be devastating.

Minimized span of control. With this style of management, an individual can only safely manage an organization with the number of people they can see and direct most of the time. They put a ceiling on how many people they can oversee and how big their span of control can be.

<u>Frustration and demotivation of the team.</u> We were created with the need and desire for freedom. When you are not properly empowered to do what you're capable of doing and passionate about doing, you're left sitting around waiting for the next instruction from the owner or boss. When the boss isn't around to give instructions, people get frustrated. The team is not motivated because they're treated more like children than adults.

<u>Lack of initiative and creativity.</u> Where micromanagement exists, initiative and creativity disappear from the organization. In a larger organization where you have a micromanager, think about the vast amount of creativity and initiative that is wasted and the cost to the organization of not having that.

Moses' father-in-law Jethro paid the family a visit and noticed what was going on. He said, "What you are doing is not good, and you will wear yourself out and the people too." He recommended that Moses share the workload. Moses had been using personal and positional power, but Jethro was suggesting he use organizational power. He suggested creating an organization chart and sharing the work with able and trusted leaders.

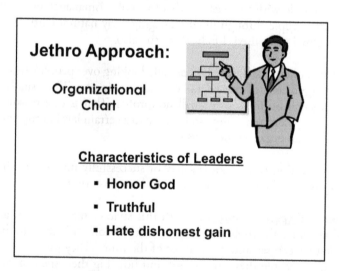

When you share the workload with competent and willing people, you significantly increase the number of people you can reach with your management or leadership style.

How do you let go without losing control?

A typical comment from an autocratic manager is, "If I let go, I will lose control." They don't understand it is possible to share the power but still keep control. Neither do they understand an autocrat can never have control of more than about five people in their area of supervision. You can only micromanage what you can see and touch. Everything else going on is beyond your seeing, hearing, and direct influence.

Let's look at organizational power through the lens of this diagram:

We can learn a lot from nature about how the world is designed and is supposed to work. I really like the illustration of a river. I compare rivers to swamps to make a distinction. What are the similarities between an effective organization and a typical river?

Rivers have a current which causes movement. So do organizations. The movement in an organization comes from its vision, priorities, and goals at all levels. Goals not only give movement, but they give direction to everyone in the organization. There are other factors that give direction in organizational life as well, as previously illustrated.

The banks control the direction of the river. Rivers flow in the path of least resistance to their ultimate destination.

Organizations have boundaries as well. They are created by training, operating manuals, best practices, policies and procedures, values and culture, and ultimately enabling control systems. What happens if you change any of the following?

- Mission
- Values and culture
- Policies and procedures
- Operating manual
- Training
- Enabling control systems
- Vision, priorities, or goals

Of course, if you change any of these significantly, you impact the direction or results of the organization.

What if you change the people in the organization? You can change the people without changing the direction of the organization, unless they are the top leaders. You can also change the people without significantly impacting the results, as long as they are competent for their roles. The organizational structure and institutional boundaries create movement and maintain direction.

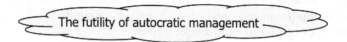

The futility of autocratic management

Look at the preceding river diagram for a few minutes and think deeply about it. In an organization of any size, think about the future with autocratic management, or even worse, micromanagement. Autocratic managers think that if they can intervene in a series of processes and give people real-time directions that require real time action, then they are in control. They are impacting the activities of the two or three people they can interact with in real time. They feel good. They feel powerful. They feel they are getting something done because they can make a decision and see an immediate or near immediate result. But if you have an organization with tens, hundreds, or thousands of people, that interaction with a handful is not changing the system. In fact, the autocrat's intervention may be messing up the system and the priorities of the people they are interacting with. That doesn't mean you should stop interacting with people. Leaders interact with people all the time. However, most of the time, the interaction is in answering questions and clearing the way for them to do their work. It's not real-time hands-on management.

Look at the diagram for a moment. Think about the organization and river comparison. If you narrow the banks of the river too much, what happens? Flooding! If you make the river too broad, what happens? A river looks more like a swamp. We will look at these realities in the next chapter.

Chapter 9

Organizational Floods and Swamps

**If you don't set the organizational boundaries right,
then you can get stagnation and damage.**

Organizational Floods

Organizational floods occur when there's too much activity going on relative to the organizational structure and boundaries. Organizational floods have two possible causes.

Too many activities or initiatives. The organization is trying to do too much. Or there's a change-oriented, idea-of-the-month type leader trying to push too much change through the existing institutional boundaries. In these cases, the leader and others work around the boundaries. Organizational flooding occurs.

The boundaries are too narrow. As organizations get more sophisticated and larger, they tend to have more policies and procedures, operating manuals, and control systems. The personality types that develop such documents and systems typically like to increase controls. As the organization grows, the people leading it don't like to get involved in that detail work and things get out of balance. The boundaries get too tight relative to the leadership's goals. People have aggressive goals they are trying to achieve. When they can't achieve them working through the established organizational boundaries, they begin to work around them. When this occurs, the very things that are supposed to stop bad behavior, protect the organization, and make it more efficient get ignored. Just like floods damage their surroundings, so does organizational flooding.

The solution

We talked about the cause of organizational flooding. Now let's talk about the cure.

First, make sure the organization has clear, focused, and unchanging priorities. If there are too many priorities, unclear priorities, or constantly changing priorities, that is a prescription for disaster. For them to be real priorities, they must be limited to a few. They need to be clearly communicated, shared with the teams, and converted into goals the teams eagerly accept. Finally, they need to be consistent and not frequently changing.

Second, establish appropriate boundaries, just like the banks of a river. The boundaries need to be balanced with the amount of work being done and the amount of change occurring.

The highest risk of organizational flooding occurs when the organization is led by charismatic change-agent leaders with boundaries established by over-controlling managers. A train wreck will occur.

Organizational swamps

About halfway through my career, I was minding my own business leading the Internal Audit Department for the company. The CEO got unhappy with another corporate department and asked me to assume leadership. I was initially proud because I assumed the leadership of the company thought I was very talented. It turned out that particular department was what I call an organizational swamp.

Real swamps stink, mainly because of the stagnation. They are dangerous because of the creatures. And they are stale because the water is not moving. Metaphorically speaking, we had all of those things in this departmental swamp.

There are three primary causes of organizational swamps.

No vision. Scripture says where there is no vision, the people perish. Without vision, there is no hope for a better future. People can't see what's ahead. They are left to deal with their fears and inhibitions.

No clear priorities. Without a clear set of priorities, people are left to figure out what matters on their own. In this particular department, since they served hospitals throughout the company, they were left to the whims of around 300 CEOs.

This department built hospitals, and there was a tendency for each one to be custom designed around the taste and ego of the CEO. To make matters worse, some CEOs weren't still at the hospital by the time it was completed.

No organizational boundaries. There weren't good policies and procedures and guidelines. The people in the department got caught between trying to do what they thought was right for the company and pleasing everyone that called in. One year, $3 million was spent on custom design architectural plans that did not have any chance of being constructed. We worked through the system all the way up to the group president level and established some very simple but straightforward guidelines on approvals necessary before drawings were started. Going forward, that saved over $3 million per year. Not only that, it saved CEOs the frustration and time of working with the architects on plans that weren't going to be approved.

The people in the construction department were always afraid of saying no to a CEO. When appropriate policies and procedures were put in place, it gave them protection and gave CEOs guidance. The company departmental surveys actually improved for this department after these boundaries were put in place.

The cure

The cure was to zero base, to get clear about the mission, and to establish some values of how we would work together. We created a vision of building the best hospitals in the nation. We established clear and consistent priorities which were translated into individual goals. Finally, we created policies and procedures to provide consistency and protect the team from customer requests without appropriate organizational approval.

Power Part I Section Questions

1. How much does your management/leader ship style resemble Moses? Jethro?

2. In what ways do you micromanage?

3. Which team members, staff, and volunteers are more interested in being controllers rather than servants? What are you doing about it?

4. Do you have any organizational flooding? Why?

5. What are some of your swampy areas? Why? What do you need to do?

POWER – PART II
INTRODUCTION

MOTIVATION

I worked in a rock quarry in the summers during college. I made minimum wage and worked long hours in very hot and dusty conditions. But I was genuinely grateful to have the job. I respected and was grateful to the manager, Vernon, who had hired me. My attitude about the job was radically different from some people who were doing the same work for the same pay as me. Over the course of four summers and doing various jobs around the quarry, I noticed more and more people doing the same work for the same pay and for the same leader, but with very different attitudes and motivations. That's when I decided there's more to motivation than just what the leader does.

The Bottom Line

- Find people who are already motivated to do what the organization needs done and who have the capability to do it. Then try not to demotivate them with any of your actions or decisions.

- Leaders inspire people while managers enforce compliance.

Chapter 10

Sources of Motivation

How much more could your organization achieve if everyone on the team was highly motivated?

Are you confused about why some of your team seems motivated while the rest doesn't? One of the more misunderstood roles of leadership relates to motivation. Walk into any room of leaders/managers and ask them for a definition of motivation. I've always gotten pretty diverse answers. Ask them about their responsibility for motivation, and you get even more diverse opinions. Is the leader responsible for motivating the team? Most people I've asked say yes. Most leaders say yes. Yet most leaders acknowledge being frustrated by not having a highly motivated workforce.

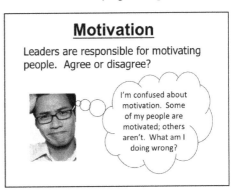

Motivation

Leaders are responsible for motivating people. Agree or disagree?

I'm confused about motivation. Some of my people are motivated; others aren't. What am I doing wrong?

61

Let's break this down and see how motivation really works. We will answer these questions:

- **What is motivation?**

- **What causes it?**

- **How does the leader influence it?**

Why was I motivated to work for minimum wage in a rock quarry? I was raised on a dairy farm. We milked cows twice a day, every day. I got up at 4:30 in the morning. We finished the evening milking usually around 6:00 p.m. In the summers, we often worked more after that. I love that I was raised on a farm, and there is much about it I liked and still miss. But it was not how I wanted to make a living. It was not what I felt called to do. My goal was to work in a business environment. I decided at an early age to take that direction. There was something inside me pulling that way. It wasn't someone else's influence but what I wanted that drove me.

As a kid, I thought this was my goal just because I wanted to be cool in the summer and warm in the winter, which the office job offered. Years later I discovered my goal was based on far more than that. I have a real passion for organizations and for working with people. Nevertheless, my goals to get a college education and work in business drove me to work hard at the rock quarry and appreciate the opportunity. For me, that job was a means to an end. For some, it was a transitional job. For others, it felt like the end.

I realized from experience that it is possible, and even likely, for leaders to have some people working for them who are motivated and others who are not. So I've always been bothered by the number of leadership trainers and written sources that emphasize leaders' responsibility for motivating people. Some people in leadership roles universally have highly motivated people while others universally have unmotivated people. I will sort through all of that later.

For my baseline understanding, I went to the Bible to understand motivation. In Scripture, I saw three sources of motivation:

- Love
- Desires of the heart
- Pain or fear of discipline

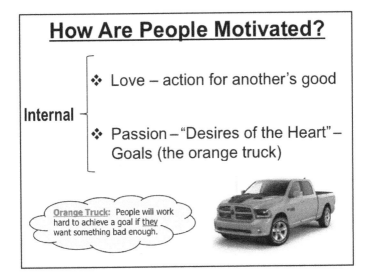

Love

I deal with leaders in a number of nonprofit ministries. The most outstanding among them have people who serve others from the depths of their hearts out of love. These people do amazing things. Yet it's not only people in nonprofit organizations that have this capacity. There are numerous CEOs, leaders, and others in for-profit organizations that also pursue a mission of providing a good or service out of love for the people they serve. The examples I can think of from my years at HCA are too numerous to mention.

Remember the story about three people laying bricks from the first section of this book? I'm often asked by people in organizations how to get people to move from being bricklayers to builders to cathedral builders. The key is love. Until people care deeply and passionately about something and someone beyond themselves, they will not have the vision of a cathedral builder.

What does this have to do with influencing the motivation of a team? Very simply, people are motivated when you place them in positions where they can do the things they love doing because they love and want to serve others.

After the flood of May 2010 in Nashville that affected my home, one of the hourly workers that came to help was a lady named Janine. She showed up at my house one Saturday morning after working two weeks straight at sixteen hours a day without a break. This was her first day off since the flood. She said she woke up early Saturday morning and remembered something about my house that she wanted to check to see if there was moisture. She checked, and indeed there was moisture and mold in a spot that others would have missed. I had a long talk with Janine, trying to understand her motivation for the hours she put it in and why she took part of her day off to help me. She said, "I just love helping people." As we talked further, it was obvious to me she was a person of faith who loved God deeply and, therefore, was able to love others as well. This is the kind of person it takes to be a cathedral builder. Her motive was love.

Desires of the heart

Psalm 37:4 speaks of God granting His servants the "desires of your heart." There are many places in Scripture that talk about the desires of the heart. Proverbs 4:23 says that out of the heart come the "issues of life." What is the heart? It is the seat of decision making, our will, and our emotions. What is a desire of the heart? In simple terms, it's something we desire deeply. I remember when I was a young boy living on the farm, and I wanted a pony. I wanted one so badly that I asked my dad about it every week until he finally gave me one. There was nothing noble or self-sacrificing about this desire. It was just something I wanted deeply enough to keep asking my dad until he decided, out of love, to give it to me.

I remember well when I had a hard time finding an approach to get my teenage son interested in any kind of work. Then one day, he started talking about an orange International Scout truck he wanted to buy.

He already had a vehicle I had bought for him that was better than the Scout. I told him if he wanted the Scout, he should get a job and earn the money to pay for it. He went to work for a landscaping crew and worked really hard all summer to make the money to buy the Scout. At that time, it was a great desire of his heart, and he was willing to do what it took to get it.

With great desire goes great effort. Dan Miller, in *No More Dreaded Mondays*,[5] recommends figuring out what makes you mad, glad, or sad. His thinking is that if something invokes a great emotion in you, such as some injustice that makes you mad, or some need of other people that makes you sad, or something you want that gives you a deep gladness, you will be highly motivated to act on that emotion. In biblical terms, it is a desire of your heart.

What do the people on your team care deeply and passionately about? If they are in positions that let them do what they love to do, you will have good, solid builders. If they do it for the sake of others, you will have cathedral builders.

Discipline/Pain

The final motivation Scripture refers to is discipline or pain. In Deuteronomy 30:15-20 (and surrounding chapters), God outlined His requirements for blessings and also the curses that would result if His people did not follow His ways. Throughout the Old Testament, God's prophets were sent to His people when they strayed to warn them of coming judgment if they did not change direction. Judgment or pain was used by God in dealing with His people to change their behavior, but only as a last resort and after much patience.

Now think about this in organizational life. With what type of people do you most frequently need to invoke some discipline or pain? Isn't it the bricklayers? Isn't it the ones there just for the money, just because they need a job? Isn't it all drudgery to them? Remember, what is drudgery to one person might be a great joy to another who loves to help people.

My suggestion is that if you have people on the team who constantly need discipline, they would be happier in another organization or in another role.

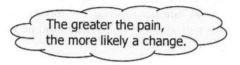

The greater the pain, the more likely a change.

Country comedian Jerry Clower expresses this idea very well. He tells the story of coon hunting with his cousin Marcel. They treed what they thought was a coon, and Marcel climbed the tree to shake it out. He soon discovered they had treed a bobcat, not a coon. The bobcat squalled, and Marcel screamed. This went on for quite some time. Finally, Marcel yelled to Jerry, "Just shoot up in here amongst us. One of us has got to have some relief." Marcel was a man desperate for something to change. We would say he was highly motivated.

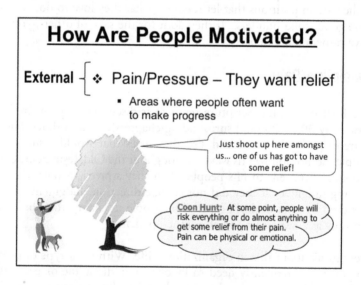

If pain, physical or emotional, causes us to want to change something, are we motivated every time we feel pain? Let's take a common issue for lots of people, myself included. Are you happy with your weight? Are you happy with your overall health and how much you work out? Most people I know would say no. Yet most people are not distressed enough to change. Therefore, we would say they are not motivated. They are just unhappy at this point. Marcel fought with the bobcat for a while before he began experiencing enough pain to tell Jerry to shoot up into the tree.

Most people get motivated to go on a diet or start exercising the day they stand in front of a mirror, observe themselves, and either break into tears or (worse) a string of profanities and say something along the lines of "I can't stand this anymore." That level of emotion is usually required to take some action.

When I was a kid, my favorite cartoon was Popeye. In every episode, the villain, Brutus, would push Popeye to his limits. Just before Popeye would eat his spinach so he could be strong enough to defeat Brutus, he said: "I have stands all I can stands, and I can't stands no more." That's when Popeye would take drastic action to make everything right. We tend to be motivated when we can't stand how things are anymore. Often this comes from emotional or physical pain.

Chapter 11

Impacting Motivation

> **Do you know the ways you impact motivation positively as a leader and how you may destroy it?**

Motivation comes from inside a person. That doesn't mean a manager or leader can't have an impact. Good leaders tend to impact a person's motivation positively, and weak managers often impact their motivation negatively.

SET GOALS

What does this look like in our personal and organizational lives? Brian Tracy says to set goals that are like heat-seeking missiles. I've always been a goal setter by nature. It comes from my "D"–dominant personality. But Tracy had a significant impact on me as a young professional in setting goals and using them in organizational life. I've learned through experience that if you can understand people's goals, you can begin to understand what they do—like my son when he wanted the

International Scout. When I helped people set goals they agreed to and believed in, it impacted their performance.

A key to leaders' influencing motivation is knowing what people want. Leaders can help illuminate wants and needs people already have. This is an appropriate thing to do to influence motivation.

When I led the Internal Audit Department for HCA, I spent considerable time illuminating the passions, dreams, and goals among the team. Sometimes people's passions and dreams get buried. They've been hurt or failed at some point in life and are just trying to survive, so they put their dreams on hold. Sometimes dreams and passions are ignored or forgotten. People get busy doing what's necessary and forget about doing what they dream about or are passionate about.

Sometimes people just can't see their potential. I spent a lot of time working with people, identifying their potential, and "calling it out" in them. I told them they were setting their sights too low. They didn't have enough self-esteem or enough confidence. Sometimes I pointed people in a different direction because they didn't have good self-awareness.

Set High Expectations

Through the experience of having parents and being a parent, I know firsthand the impact of expectations on people. In my family, we were expected to work hard. We did, and it just seemed normal. In my wife's family, they did a lot of things to please and meet the expectations of other people. That thinking was so ingrained in her that she still does it to this day. When I ask her why she's doing something, her response is often based on what somebody else expects. The expectations I had of my children have impacted them significantly.

In society, I see the impact of expectations on people. There are for-profit businesses and nonprofit organizations that have cultures of high expectation. By contrast, there are those that have cultures of low expectation, resulting in mediocrity.

Encourage Them

A young boy named Frank once brought a Christmas present to school for his teacher, Mrs. Jones. She opened her gifts in front of the students. When she opened Frank's gift, the other kids laughed. It was a partially used bottle of perfume. Frank was obviously embarrassed because of the laughter of the other kids, but Mrs. Jones thanked him for it and made over it like it was a fine gift, even though she didn't quite understand.

A bit later, when none of the other students were around, Mrs. Jones asked Frank how he chose that particular gift. Tears came to his eyes as he explained it was his mom's perfume. He had given it to his mom last Christmas because he knew it was her favorite perfume. His mom was very sick that Christmas, but she always used it and thanked Frank for it. She passed away a few months later. Frank told Mrs. Jones he hoped she liked it as much as his mom did and wanted her to have it so she would smell like his mom.

Mrs. Jones then took a special interest in Frank. She found out about his home life, which was tough. His father did the best he could but was poor and had to work long hours, leaving Frank to fend for himself. Mrs. Jones began to look at Frank differently. She determined she would encourage, support, and love him. In the final half of his fourth-grade year, Frank went from being a poor student to a very good student. In the years that followed, Frank would always go by and see Mrs. Jones every year and tell her how he was doing. He was making A's every year. At some point he moved away, and she didn't see him anymore.

A few years later, she got a note from Frank. He had just graduated from high school with honors, and he wrote to Mrs. Jones thanking her for the difference she made in his life. Four years later, she got another note from Frank. He had just graduated from college at the top of his class. A few years later, she got another note thanking her for the impact the she had on his life. He had just finished medical school and was now a doctor.

Leaders often underestimate the impact for both bad and good they can have on people within their sphere of influence. When we take a personal interest in people, understand their background and challenges, and go the extra mile to meet some of their personal needs, it can leave a deep impression. Often, it doesn't take anything heroic to make a big difference in someone's life.

I remember the going-away party the team threw for me when I left the Internal Audit Department at HCA for a different role. A grown man stood with tears in his eyes telling a story I had forgotten. I began to remember some of the details as he told the story. I was on vacation and made a call to a hospital CEO to recommend this fellow for a CFO position, which he got. That move was a stepping stone to other career moves that turned out really well for him. I thought nothing of it and had long since forgotten it. But because I took some time early in the morning while on vacation to help advance his career, it made a deep impression on this man. It required very little of me. I had forgotten about it, but it made a great difference to him.

I believed I had a great team at HCA.
Some people disagreed with me.
That didn't matter.
What mattered most was that I believed it,
and my team believed it.
That made the team better
because we believed it.

Provide Security

I once got a call from a friend who had not worked for me for a long time. She was getting a new boss and was really nervous. She was putting a lot of pressure on herself trying to ensure she had the perfect first day. She wanted me to help her think of anything she may have forgotten. She told me what she had done to prepare, which was more than adequate. So, did I rack my brain trying to think of anything else she could have done? No, she was already very prepared. What she needed

71

was not a longer to-do list. She needed confidence. She needed a sense of security.

So what did I do? I gave her confidence and security. I reminded her she was the best person in her role that I knew from a very long career. I reminded her of the background the new leader was coming from and that she was better than what he'd been used to. I told her if there was anything else he wanted, she would be more qualified to get it quickly than anyone else. By the time I finished explaining to her the confidence I had in her and how well-prepared she was, she was very calm and settled. Had I simply added to her list, she would have been even more prepared but still anxious and insecure. People are more creative and do a better job when they are calm and secure. They make mistakes when they are nervous and scared.

Sometimes, when employees ask if there's anything else they can do for you, they are not seeking more work. They are seeking affirmation and security. If you have hired good employees, you have put yourself in the perfect position to be affirming from the heart when employees feel insecure. And it is crucial in affirming employees that you be genuine. The best employees can spot a fake affirmation from a long distance.

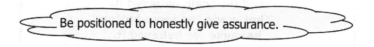
Be positioned to honestly give assurance.

One way to ensure you can continually give employees the affirmation they need is to hire great people. When you take shortcuts in the interview process or hire somebody just to fill a position quickly, you are not confident you have the right person. If you make a poor choice in hiring or in delegating a particular project, you will start to have doubts about the person's ability to get the job done. When you have doubts, you cannot maintain your integrity and give employees assurances that they can do the job.

Esteem Them

In our culture, we talk much about self-esteem. But we don't spend as much time talking about showing honor to others. We like to be thought well of. We like to be valued. It's a basic need people have. And the Bible affirms that need. It teaches us to think of others more highly than ourselves (Philippians 2:3-4). Of course, all people of all ages need to be esteemed. But I've noticed as people mature in professional life, being esteemed takes on more value.

> *"Give preference to one another in honor."*
> *Romans 12:10*

As a practical matter, how do we do this? Really, it's quite simple. Hire people that are more gifted for and joyful about their jobs than you are. Then, you can appreciate their talent and their willingness to do work you are not suited for and don't like doing.

I know people in various organizations who would trade blocks of their compensation package to be genuinely esteemed by the organization's leadership. The mistake we make in organizational life, and that I've made, is to show appreciation and esteem to people only when the results are good. We tend to show esteem most when people need it least. Think about it. People know they're doing well and feel good when the results are positive. It is when results are not positive that people need to be esteemed the most.

I remember a turnaround situation in which I was involved. I was working my hardest, being my most creative, and doing some of the best work of my career. In most situations, a lot of hard work and good planning happen a long time before results turn. That's where I was. But the corporate bureaucrats, not the top leaders, constantly made life hard on me. That reminded me of the time on the family farm when I was carrying a 100-pound feed sack, and my much smaller brother hit me at the knees. I went down, of course. You can't carry that much weight, be hit at the knees, and stay on your feet. My little brother did not know or care about that at the time. We expect better out of our leaders. But we don't always get it.

I remember vividly how it felt to be carrying such heavy weight during that turnaround and how unfair it felt for others to be piling on. If I had been lazy or doing the wrong thing, corporate bureaucrats' involvement and follow-up could have been constructive. But since I wasn't doing anything wrong, their negativity took time away from important activities, caused me to work longer hours under more stress than was necessary, and influenced me to have far less respect for those who were choosing to make life hard.

> *"That I may be encouraged together*
> *with you while among you."*
> **Romans 1:12**

After many months of some of the hardest and best work I had done in my career, the results started to turn around. Then people started bragging on me. They said glowing things about me. I was relieved due to the lack of pressure, but the accolades from "other people" meant nothing to me. They were not really esteeming me. They were happy over the results and giving me all the credit. I wasn't due all the credit any more than I was due all the blame earlier. When things smoothed out, I wasn't working nearly as hard, as smart, or as creatively as I had been months earlier. But I was bragged on more for my hard work and intelligence than at any other time in my career.

What's wrong with this picture? I was doing my hardest and best work under constant criticism when I most needed to be esteemed and feel some sense of security. When the results changed and I felt good and secure based on the results, unneeded flattery and praise were abundant.

The situation reminds me of a TV interview with Jeff Fisher, former coach of the Tennessee Titans football team. Two years earlier, the Titans had come up one yard short of winning the Super Bowl. This particular year, they were having a tough season, and the TV broadcasters and fans were giving Coach Fisher a hard time. He stared into the camera and simply said, "Listen, two years ago, we came up one yard short of winning the Super Bowl. We haven't forgotten how to coach." In the experience I described earlier, I had worked for the company for over 17 years. It wasn't like my critics didn't know me, my capabilities, or my past contributions. The bureaucrats (not the top leaders) who unleashed on me seemed not to care.

I have to admit that even after that experience, I found myself doing the same thing to others at times. When we are under pressure and trying to get things done, or when we are focused on our own image and reputation, it's easy to forget what other people need. Our default mode is to tell people what we want and expect, and to blame them when the results aren't there. We have to think about what other people need most in the present circumstances. Often that requires us to do something or say something the opposite of what we feel like saying at the time. I'm not suggesting you ever lie or mislead people about what you are thinking. I'm simply suggesting that sometimes we need to think more clearly. We give people an assignment because we think they can do it based on their past. If they truly can't do it, we are most at fault for delegating it to them and should point the finger at ourselves first.

If we've done a good job delegating, we should believe in the people to whom we gave the assignment, give them reasonable freedom, and follow up at reasonable intervals. Most importantly, when the assignment is really challenging, we should remember to encourage them and show our esteem for them as valuable members of the team.

The Pastor's Wife

All people need to be esteemed. Their role in life doesn't eliminate the need. It's surprising at times the people who don't receive the esteem they should. A pastor's wife had a birthday party. She and her husband had served faithfully in ministry their whole lives. They had served one church for 20 years. The lady was a widow, and some church friends were throwing her an 80th birthday party. She happened to comment how much she appreciated the party. Her next comment wasn't stated negatively but was quite a surprise. She said she had never had a party or recognition just for her. Everything else in her life had been associated with her pastor husband or the church. She was genuinely touched because at 80 years old, her church friends had a birthday party just for her.

Christmas Barbecue

Gizmo worked at the rock quarry. He wore steel-toe boots, a hard hat, and dusty clothes like everyone else who worked there. Every year, we had a Christmas barbecue lunch at the quarry. Everyone else wore their steel-toe boots, hard hats, and dusty clothes, but not Gizmo. Gizmo wore a suit and tie. As a college kid observing this for the first time, it struck me as really odd. So I asked the foreman, "What's the deal with Gizmo?" He told me that one year Gizmo dressed up a little bit for the lunch. Jim, the manager of the rock quarry, bragged on him and commented on how good he looked. Every year since then, Gizmo put on a suit and tie for the Christmas barbecue. Gizmo needed to feel important. He needed to stand out. He very deeply needed to be esteemed. The comments he got at the Christmas lunch may have been the most significant affirmation he received the whole year.

Ways to Give Esteem

One of the most impactful ways of showing esteem is to write a personal note or letter. It doesn't have to be long, but it needs to be sincere, personal, and specific to the person. I remember a guy who worked for me several years and moved twice in the process. I wrote him a personal handwritten letter thanking him for some specific contributions to the company. Years later, he talked about the letter in front of a group of people. He teared up as he said it was the first letter he ever received in his life thanking him for anything. The tragedy is that he was in his mid to late 50s when I wrote the letter.

I've seen two different men tear up from something I wrote. The first was when I was a young manager and had written a curt note on a report from an employee. I happened to walk by his office as he was reading the note and saw the hurt on his face. That was over 30 years ago.

It was the first time I had ever written a note like that, and it was the last. I never wanted to be responsible for making someone feel that way again. The second man I saw tear up over something I wrote was the one to whom I wrote the nice note. When I saw that, I thought about how many years I had been a leader and how many opportunities I had missed to show esteem to others or to bring them joy.

Think about it. How many personal notes have you received in your life where someone showed you esteem? How many of them have you thrown away? I've never thrown any of mine away and don't plan to. That's the difference they make. It may be one of the easiest yet most highly impactful things leaders can do.

Hire the Right People

So, what is the leader's role in motivation? Very broadly, it is to hire people who are already motivated; to help illuminate their passions, dreams, and goals; to help align their goals with the organization's needs; and to try not to demotivate them. That's easier said than done. How do we accomplish this? It starts with the hiring process. We need to hire people with the following characteristics:

- Right personality profile. If we hire people who are going to be "swimming against the current" of their natural personalities, they will be frustrated and demotivated from the beginning.

- Right talent and experience. Hire people who want to do the job and know how to do the job.

- Desire to make a difference – "cathedral builders." I had dinner with an old friend recently who I could tell was really tired. When he described his last few weeks' schedule, I understood why. I thought he might be frustrated with his job and ready to quit. Yet that wasn't the case at all. As I listened to him, it was clear he had a great vision for the impact he could have on the company and the quality of healthcare people received. He was passionate about making a difference and was willing to push himself to the limits to achieve his goals.

- <u>Ability to use their talents and pursue their passions and "calling"</u> by doing what they want to do while helping your organization meet its objectives.

  o Can this person do what you need them to do because they want to do it?

  o Can they embrace the values and culture of your organization?

  o Can they enjoy working with your people?

  o Would they do this job without a paycheck if money were no object for them?

WARNING

Don't demotivate them by:

- Lack of clear goals and priorities

- Lack of measurement and feedback

- Micromanaging

- Poor hiring

Chapter 12

What Motivates Millennials?

> **How much stronger would your organization be if you knew what motivates Millennials?**

There's a great difference, according to Kent Wessinger's research, between how Millennials see themselves and how the BXers (Baby Boomers and Generation X) see them.[6] The difference suggests what motivates Millennials.

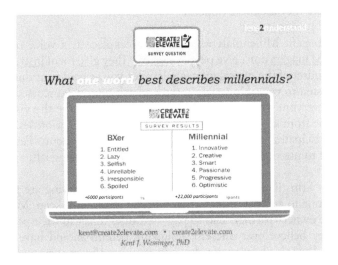

The following graphic shows what traditional employers are doing to retain Millennials and what Millennials find important as job retention factors.[7]

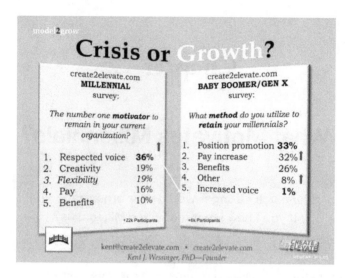

Millennials change jobs on average every 18 months. That's because it takes them a year to figure out they're going to be unhappy going forward with the current employer and about six months to find another job where they are more hopeful.

A key benefit Millennials want in the workplace is a voice or to be heard. Managers don't give people a voice. They give them instructions. The mindset of the typical manager is, once you've paid your dues, then I will listen to you. However, in the leadership model discussed in this book, everyone gets a voice. Ideas on how to achieve the vision are welcome from anyone. People are given input on the priorities. Everyone participates in setting goals they are passionate about. People are allowed to use their creativity in how they achieve their goals.

Services firms like tax, accounting, legal, and engineering are particularly prone to an environment that will not attract and keep Millennials. The owners/partners had to pay their dues to get to their positions, and they believe everyone else following behind should have to pay theirs. They think everyone else is as motivated by money as they are.

Thus, Millennial turnover is high. Service firms that understand how to engage and keep Millennials will end up with an opportunity to buy other firms or simply take their business over time by having the best retention rate and best people. This is a great opportunity for the savvy firm owner.

Clear-cut, measurable goals allow for flexibility in a number of job settings, though it is more difficult in some service industries. There's one technology company that only requires people to be in the office four hours per day. They can do the rest of the work from any location. The most productive time of the day for many Millennials is from 12 a.m. to 3 a.m. When you can track results rather than just micromanage, the leader can tell if the work is getting done.

Nobody likes criticism, but Millennials respond especially negatively to criticism. Remember, this is the generation that got a trophy just for showing up. In a managerial environment where they're being judged and all the exceptions are pointed out as errors, they are not going to respond well at all.

In the leadership environment I advocate, mistakes are seen as learning opportunities and <u>leaders</u> <u>coach</u> to help employees get better rather than just judging and criticizing. Millennials like to learn. They are more open to being mentored than any other generation. They will respond well to being led in an environment that:

- Changes so they can use their creativity

- Keeps score so they can know how they're doing

- Celebrates and rewards results

- Coaches to correct

- Only uses discipline as a last resort

I believe everyone responds better in that kind of environment, but especially Millennials. **I will say it again: Millennials will not be managed, but they will respond to true leadership as good as or better than any generation.**

Power – Part II, Motivation
Section Questions

1. How are you trying to influence motivation?
   Love, vision and passion, pain?

2. Of the ways you can influence motivation,
   which ones do you need to work on?

3. Does your team feel secure? Esteemed?

4. When did you last write someone a handwrit
   ten note of appreciation?

5. Who do you need to write now?

PEOPLE
INTRODUCTION

What a difference one person can make!

Early in my experience of leading the Physician Services organization for HCA, I had a hodgepodge of people, all of whom were already there when I got the job. Many fit their jobs well, but a number didn't. One division got more complaints than all the other 12 divisions of the company. So I knew I needed somebody new to lead that division. To my good fortune, I met a man named Louis. He had superb experience in the field, and his personality profile was a great match. This rarely happens, but 15 minutes into the interview I just knew he was my guy. I completed the interview early and offered him the job on the spot.

About 18 months later, I got more unsolicited compliments about that division then all 12 of the other divisions in the company. Truly, what a difference one guy made!

The Bottom Line

- You must have the right people in the right positions to make progress.

- Unless you evaluate the whole person in the hiring process, you are <u>using</u> them instead of <u>engaging</u> them as a <u>partner</u>. People who know you are using them do not become cathedral builders.

- <u>People</u> <u>follow</u> real <u>leaders</u> <u>willingly</u>. <u>People</u> <u>comply</u> with <u>managers</u>.

Chapter 13

Picking the Team

> **How much more fun would leadership be if you chose your team well?**

I've often heard it said that management would be fine if not for the people. On the contrary, I learned over many years how fun leadership can be when you have the right people. There are three common problems organizations have in putting the right people in the right places.

- A great number of people, even in large and sophisticated organizations, are not good at hiring. They don't use a consistent process in evaluating candidates.

- While a lot of organizations use personality profiles to understand the uniqueness of the people they are interviewing, a great number don't. The incremental cost and opportunity cost of not getting the right people is huge. (We devote a separate chapter to this.)

85

- When the wrong person is put into the job or when things change and the person no longer fits the job, many organizations are not good at dealing with unsatisfactory performance. Some organizations are too quick to terminate people and are rather brutal about the exit. Many others try to be compassionate but drag the process out too long, which hurts the individual and organization.

We will deal with these common issues in the next few pages.

Picking the Team

We played ball at recess when I was a kid in grade school. Two people always identified themselves as leaders and chose teams. One would choose a player, and then the other would choose. This continued until everyone was chosen. The best players were chosen first and the weakest players last. You always knew how good people thought you were based on how soon you were chosen. The process actually worked quite well in choosing talent. The leaders had observed you playing and knew what you were capable of. They assigned positions on the field based on their observation of people's aptitude for those positions. Though this entire process was informal, the kids who were leaders did a good job of identifying talent and putting people in the right positions so the teams were fairly evenly matched.

We finish school, go to college, get a job, and then get frustrated with this process of choosing people. It seemed so simple when we were in grade school. Why is that? We had multiple chances to observe the talent of the individuals over time before we chose them to be on our team.

When we hire people outside the organization, they come to an interview with a résumé and a game face. We have not had the opportunity to observe them, nor do we know which position they play best. At the end of the interview, what we really know is how they come across in an interview. Plus, individuals and companies are making a living teaching people how to prepare for and handle interviews to get the job they want. Candidates are coming to the interview with great preparation. They are better at controlling the interview process than many executives who conduct the interviews.[8]

Let's look at what a good recruiting process looks like.

Define The Successful Candidate — The 5 P's

It's hard to make good hires consistently unless you know exactly what you're looking for. It's important to define who the successful candidate will be in terms of what I call the five P's:

PURPOSE – *What were they created to do and accomplish?* Some people refer to this as calling. Generally, this is what a person does best and something they love doing. Frequently, other people point out how good they are at a certain thing.

PERSONALITY – *What is their hardwiring?* This is their unique personality profile, which gives great indicators about what they will be successful doing and what they will not like and may not be able to do.

PASSION – *What do they care deeply about?* Someone may have the personality profile to do a certain job, but they may have no passion for it.

PREPARATION – *What is their preparation for this job?* This includes all life experiences that may impact their ability to be successful in this job. It also includes their education and training, as well as any other jobs they've had to this point. My pastor says his best preparation to lead a megachurch was working with his dad in his TV store, learning how to deal with the public.

POTENTIAL – *What is their ability to grow in the job and with the organization?* Many organizations are dynamic and growing. They want people who can grow with the organization.

The Search

It's hard to hit a target if you don't have a painted bull's-eye. Beginning the search is the next step in the process once you have a clear perspective on what you're looking for in terms of the five P's. Many people simply create a newspaper or newsletter ad to gather résumés. That's perfectly OK. However, I wasn't necessarily looking for people that didn't have jobs or who were dissatisfied with the jobs they had. I was looking for the best in the industry. Therefore, while I did use advertisements, I spent a good deal of time being proactive and searching for the candidate I wanted. Many times, they weren't looking for a job. Knowing clearly what you're looking for helps in the process of determining where and how you will look for the right candidate.

Interview and Close

The final step in the process is the interview and close. Many leaders have a natural tendency to want to close too quickly without doing an adequate interview. An adequate interview includes looking at the whole person—all five P's.

Many managers rush through interviews without spending adequate time preparing for them and the candidates being interviewed. Some of this is based on our ego. We want the right of first refusal. Therefore, we tell them a lot about the job and try to make sure they are interested before asking our questions. This just gives them ammunition to tell us what they think we want to hear.

One time early in my career, I had a job candidate say all of the sudden, "That sounds great. When do I start?" I was embarrassed and realized I had not even interviewed him. I had asked very few questions and didn't know if I wanted to offer him the job or not. The best approach is to develop a consistent interview guide that you use on all candidates. Ask your questions first. Then answer their questions about the job.

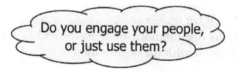

Do you engage your people, or just use them?

Businesses tend to focus on a person's preparation. They want to know if the person can do the job and is willing to do the job for the pay they offer. Ministries often look at a person's purpose or calling and their preparation. If you don't look at the whole person through the lens of the five P's, you're likely using them rather than engaging them.

Interview Guide

To pick wisely, you need a strong and consistent interview process. I like to develop questions around three categories:

I. Pre-Résumé
II. Preparation/Résumé
III. Post-Résumé

This is illustrated in the diagram below:

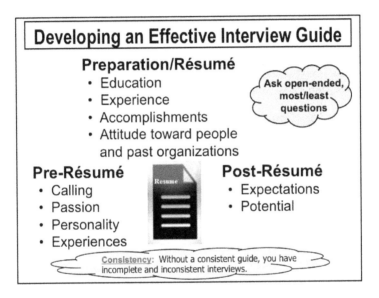

Pre-Résumé

In the pre-résumé phase, we want to know about their understanding of their calling or purpose in life. What have they always been naturally good at? What have people always gone to them for because of their special talent in that area? Take time to understand their passions, what they care deeply about. You can determine a person's calling best by asking probing questions about what makes them glad, mad, or sad. What makes them glad leads to understanding their deepest joy. What makes them mad leads to an understanding of injustices they would like to see corrected. What makes them sad is usually lost potential for self or others. The answers to these questions should give some insight into whether the job will ignite their passions.

Use resources to understand their unique personality and hardwiring. There are a great number of personality profiles available on the open market. In chapter 17, I discuss the ones we use at Vision Leadership and why. Having this done before the interview will help you ask even more insightful questions.

Have them articulate clearly how their pre-résumé calling and work experiences prepared them for the job for which they are interviewing.

Finally, understand significant experiences that have shaped their life. For example, what influence have their family, parents, and siblings had on them? What major life experiences have influenced who they are and how they think today?

Preparation/Experience – Résumé

Their résumé should help you understand their education, work experiences, and major accomplishments. You're looking for experience and accomplishments that help you determine if they will be successful in the job you are trying to fill.

Ask about each job they had and their accomplishments in it. Ask about what they liked the most and least about each job. The process of doing this will also help you validate the accuracy of their DISC personality profile. There should be a direct correlation. Sometimes, you find the things they like least about the roles they have been in are the primary requirements for some aspects of the role you're interviewing for.

Look at the length of time between jobs and the reasons for leaving one job to pursue another. Be sure to understand why they would be motivated to leave an existing job to take the one you are offering.

Understanding their attitude toward people is huge. Many times, a person is competent for the job but either is not going to like it or is not going to be accepted by others in the workplace because of their attitude, which drives how they interact with others.

90

Ask candidates what they like most and least about peers, subordinates, and past leaders. Take your time. These discussions will give you great insights about candidates' attitudes toward other people. If your leadership style is more like one of their favorite leaders from the past, you have a better chance of a good relationship. If your style is closer to the leaders they liked least, the relationship may not work. The same is true for their peer group.

If the individuals you're hiring will supervise others, you want to understand their attitude toward subordinates. If their view is not consistent with the culture you are trying to create for your organization, you should not put them into the position. Also, ask them what their leaders, peers, and subordinates like most and least about them. This will give you a sense of their self-awareness.

I remember Frank, who was hired by someone else but eventually reported to me. Over time, I noticed that he was very critical of every person he'd ever worked for. In his mind, they were all "idiots" or "jerks." It didn't take me long to figure out that no matter what I did, that would be his final assessment of me. Sure enough, after he left my department and went to another part of the company, he began "badmouthing" me. If I had been the original hiring professional using this interviewing approach, that characteristic would have been identified during the interview, and he would not have been brought into the company.

If individuals have never liked any organization they've worked for, there is very little chance they will like your organization. I never experienced an exception to that rule. To the contrary, Frank and many others like him convinced me how reliable it is. Ask what they like most and least about the organization or company they just left or are considering leaving. Listen for aspects of the culture they liked or didn't like. Listen for policies and procedures that annoyed them. Compare these to your own organization to see if they would be any happier. Listen for a critical attitude toward the organization. If you happen to know it's a good organization and they are very critical, it could be a red flag for you. If you happen to know it's not a good organization, listen and see if they can tactfully explain what they didn't like without a critical spirit. Remember that the attitudes they have toward their former organization will come with them to your organization.

Post-Résumé

Find out about their expectations for the future. Ask questions about their compensation history. Ask what they liked most and least about their overall compensation package. This will give you an idea of what they value in a package. Some people like their salary packages with limited equity or bonus potential. Some people prefer less base play with more significant bonus or equity opportunities. Knowing this will help you structure a package that fits them best if you want to hire them.

The compensation discussion will give you an understanding of what they have become accustomed to in the past and their expectations about the future. If they have become accustomed to healthy annual increases and you're hiring them at the top end of your pay range, you already know those kinds of increases will not be possible in your organization going forward. Having a clear understanding of their compensation history and expectations will keep you from making mistakes.

Ask questions about their future aspirations and goals. Ask about their mobility. These things may give you some insights into their potential and desire to grow with your organization.

Talk more about what they think, and avoid questions they can easily answer with what they believe you want to hear. I found that an interview following this simple approach, along with a personality profile done in advance, is superior to most other approaches.

Think about their potential. Is your organization growing? Do you need them to grow with it? Is your organization stagnant? Do you need them to be willing to be satisfied with the status quo? Assess their potential to grow with the organization, if needed.

The key is it takes time, energy, and lots of listening to interview well. Leaders are typically in a hurry and do not spend the necessary time on this very important responsibility. As a result, they spend much more time dealing with the problems of not hiring the right person. Plus, they have the added costs of going through the process again trying to get the right person. A leader must prioritize interviewing and do it with excellence. It will save time, energy, and money in the long run.

Following this outline will give you a consistent interview. A challenge many managers and leaders have is they don't ask the same questions of all the candidates. Also, in ministries and nonprofits where there are typically group interviews, each interview can be radically different depending on the order of questions that come from the group and the number of follow-up questions. If the group talks to three different candidates, it's conceivable to have three radically different interviews.

Chapter 14

Poor Performance

> **How much more productive would your organization be if you had no unmotivated, poor performers?**

Sometimes leaders come to the realization, "Oh no! I have people in place who don't fit the job. I have a 'square peg in a round hole.'"

It's not uncommon for leaders to be frustrated because a number of their people don't seem to be meeting their expectations. The natural assumption of some leaders is, "I have bad people. I need to 'fire' them and get some different people." This is a simplistic and often counterproductive way to view the situation. Start by understanding the reasons for underperformance.

- Did they fit at one time, but the circumstances or work environment changed?

- Has there been a change in the people they work with and around?

94

- Has something changed in another area of their life that is impacting their performance? Is this change temporary or permanent?

- Were they ever suited for this position, or was it a bad hire?

- Has their performance actually changed, or is it my attitude toward them that has changed? Am I under a lot of stress, causing me to be more critical of the team?

When we are not seeing the results we desire out of people, the norm for many leaders is to put off doing anything and hope it gets better. A common reason for such procrastination is lack of confidence a replacement will be better. Yet hoping something will change without taking any action has less chance for success than gambling in Las Vegas.

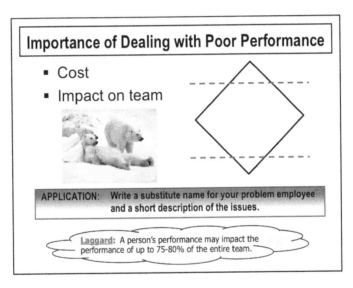

Importance of Dealing with Poor Performance

- Cost
- Impact on team

APPLICATION: Write a substitute name for your problem employee and a short description of the issues.

Laggard: A person's performance may impact the performance of up to 75-80% of the entire team.

Sometimes leaders don't deal with personnel issues as they should because the organization is meeting its objectives and they are not forced to deal with them.

Leaders have enough problems to contend with every day, so there's a tendency to deal only with the ones requiring immediate attention. But let's look at this from a stewardship standpoint. Often we are pleased when our teams are making a positive net contribution. For example, let's say the company's desired net profit is 10 percent. The team celebrates and everyone gets the bonus for delivering 10 percent. What if the potential of the team was really 20, 30, or 40 percent? Should the team be celebrating at 10 percent? Should the leader receive a bonus? Too often, leaders look merely at how well they are achieving their target and do not exercise their stewardship responsibilities to optimize what is possible with the resources available. This is a disservice to the organization and to the other members of the team.

I will take a very practical example. I go to a number of nonprofit and church gatherings. Some people leading such meetings habitually wait for the last few stragglers to come in before starting and, therefore, always start late. I am personally a stickler for showing up on time. But when I am engaged with habitually-late organizations, I find myself showing up late because I know the meeting won't start on time anyway. There's a high cost to keeping partially committed people in your organization. There's also a high cost to keeping people in positions where, for whatever reason, they are not doing a good job. Others on the team see it and, either consciously or subconsciously, it impacts their commitment and effort. I've experienced this many times.

In organizational life, a few people typically are competing with each other to be best. A few are at the bottom, and the rest are somewhere in between. You impact behavior at the top by creating healthy opportunities for competition. You impact those in the middle, most of the team, by raising the bar at the bottom. GE did this by cutting their bottom 10 percent of employees every year. I'm not a proponent of that, though I do recognize it had an impact.

As stewards of the organization's resources, we have a responsibility to ensure individuals do their jobs so they do not negatively impact the attitude and effort of others.

Understanding this concept and applying it constructively changed my life as a leader. Often leaders struggle way too long with the need to make a personnel change. We let ourselves get miserable and say things we shouldn't. But even worse, we leave people in positions they don't fit.

Options for Resolution

You should do a quick, high-level assessment when you're not getting the results you want.

Look at yourself

Do you know people who are constantly critical of their staff? I do. There are some leaders that just seem to never be satisfied with the team they have. Some constantly change the team. Some keep their team but constantly complain about them. For these leaders, I have a rather harsh message: If you want a clear view of the problem, go look in a clean mirror.

I consulted with one organization where so much had been delegated to one team member—with no clear set of priorities—that he had no idea what to focus on next. Also, things had been delegated to him that did not line up with the strengths of his personality profile. Further, it would have taken two people to do the amount of work delegated to him. Guess what happened? This person, who'd been labeled a "hero" two or three years earlier, was now labeled a "bad employee" and re-leased.

The release was OK because he did not fit that job or any other the organization had at the time. But the way it was handled was not OK. The problem was not that employee, but the person he reported to. The irony was the supervisor was mad at this really good employee. Mistakes the supervisor had made were the real problem.

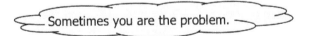

Sometimes you are the problem.

I consulted for one organization where the leader said, "I'm a great leader. I'm up to the task of coaching a world-class team. The problem is, my team is just not up to par. If the team could do their jobs as well as I can do mine, we would have a world-class organization." This guy really said that. I stood there dazed, with the words of my daughter going through my head: "Really? Really? Are you kidding me?"

You cannot be a world-class leader and say you don't have a world-class organization because your team is holding you back. You picked the team or can change it. You train the team and delegate work to them. If there's a problem with the team, you're the problem, not them. You would be surprised at how many leaders are surprised by that statement.

Do you have unrealistic expectations? Sometimes employers have really good people that have done a great job at certain things. Then the employers assume, based on past good performance, that the good people can do other things they don't have the hardwiring for. That always results in frustration and disappointment. Maybe your expectations need to change. I once consulted with a developer whose employee was very good at the paperwork and administrative aspects of closing deals. His boss also wanted him to do some of the development work. However, he simply did not have the hardwiring for that and would never have been a success in it. I advised the employer only to assign him work in accordance with his personality profile. Ten years later, they were still working together and happy with each other.

As the leader/manager, you are responsible for selecting people, training, delegating, and coaching. Assess your process, and make sure one of these areas is not the problem.

Coaching/training

Sometimes a person is struggling but can do satisfactory work if you coach them or provide them with additional training. When a performance issue arises, assume initially this is the case. In thinking through this possibility, you must determine if coaching will solve the issue and not be needed again and again. You have to think about whether a recurring problem is fair to the organization and the other individuals on the team, as well as yourself. But sometimes additional coaching and training is all that's needed.

Another position

At times a person just does not want to do what it takes to be successful in a certain role. In such instances, you have two choices: try to find them another position inside the organization or release them to find something outside the organization. Some people refer to this as firing. I like to think of it as separation—offering the individual a chance to achieve more success in another role. Some of the best hospital CFOs were poor internal auditors.

When you come to the point where you are releasing someone from your organization, think about how you would want this process to work if it were you.

Poor Strategy

Many people wait too long and hope the situation will get better. They wait until they lose their patience. They get mad or emotional, and then they take it out on the employee either verbally, with body language, or with the way they make the separation.

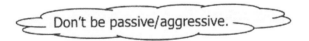

Don't be passive/aggressive.

When someone is not working out and the solution is going to be releasing them outside the organization, the sooner you make that choice the better. If you want to be gracious to the person, the sooner you decide to communicate the decision, the more time you can give them to find a job while they have a job. Or you can give them a severance package that lasts a longer period of time. Many people drag the process out six months before they finally get frustrated enough to take action. By then, they have no more patience and don't want to spend any more than they have to on the severance package. Everyone would benefit—the employer, employee, and organization—if the decisions were made sooner.

<u>Proper Strategy</u>

Here is the counseling approach regarding poor performance that most human resources departments, including HCA's, suggest. It's also what I would want if the shoe were on the other foot.

<u>Tell them the truth.</u> Objectively state there is an issue that needs to be solved. It's amazing to me the lengths to which managers will go not to have this discussion.

Help the employee understand the problem and own the solution. Be as clear as possible about the repercussions of not resolving the problem. Having employed many people over a long career, I've done my fair share of counseling people regarding their performance. People don't come to work to do a bad job, and most don't leave work at the end of the day thinking they have done a bad job. In my experience, it has been fairly common for employees who needed counseling to be unaware of the expectation gap. Many times they were ignoring the obvious, but sometimes the expectations weren't as clear as they needed to be for that employee. I tried to help them understand as clearly as possible the problem and the need to correct it.

Communicate to the employee kindly, but very plainly, that there is a problem. I've seen employees completely surprised to be terminated for poor performance. When this happens, the greatest failure is on the part of leadership, not the employee.

I have a client who spent a year dealing with someone who was not really suited for his job. In the annual review, the manager was frustrated and simply told the truth. When the employee saw how he was viewed, he quickly found another job. If this manager had been doing quarterly reviews and bringing up issues as they occurred, this could have been solved months earlier to the benefit of the employer and the employee.

If you can't come to agreement that there is an issue to be solved, then you will need to go quickly to the step of releasing the person from the organization.

Explain what happens if they can't or don't solve the issue. The answer could be they forgo raises, promotions, or bonuses. Or it could be so serious that releasing them from the organization is the answer.

Be clear at the very beginning of the process about the ramifications of the problem not being solved. Not all problems are termination offenses if not solved. There can be other repercussions to the employee that need to be understood. However, if release will be the consequence, it's especially critical that the employee knows that from the beginning.

Now the employee is in a position to determine if they can and will close the expectation gap. If they believe they can't because they don't have the skills or the motivation, they can look for a job while they still have one or resign with dignity and find something they can be successful at.

<u>**Give them a chance to fix the issue.**</u> Isn't that what you would want? Corporations usually use something they call a performance improvement plan.

Human resources at HCA suggested we have the employee create performance improvement plans to solve the problem with specific actions, timeframes, and, most importantly, results. Performance improvement plans should be more for redemptive purposes than legal protection. The key is that the employee understands the problem must be solved and that they are responsible for the resolution. It's fine and good for the leader to help the employee with the action plan. The trap I have seen many leaders step into, however, is owning the action plan themselves rather than letting the employee own it. Sometimes, the employee completes the tasks on the action plan, but the problem still exists because the leader did not make clear that the goal was resolution of the problem. The employee needs to own the action plan and the problem.

The <u>employee</u> must create an improvement plan. It's fine for the supervisor to review it and have input, but the employee must own the plan and result. Why? It's possible for employees to create long list of things they will do to solve the problem and do them, but still the issue is not resolved. Then you have to go through the whole process again.

After reviewing their plan, you should stress that it is their plan and the goal is for the issue to go away and not come back.

Giving employees the chance to develop and execute an action plan to solve the problem is as fair as you can be. Being sure they understand the consequences is also being as fair as you can be. What approach is fairer to the employee and the organization?

One reason leaders do not make changes in a timely manner is that they are scared of legal backlash. I've seen the process just discussed used many times in very difficult circumstances and have seen it be very successful. In about half the cases, the employees were able to solve the problems and continued to grow in their careers and do a good job where they were.

Sometimes employees realized on the front end they either couldn't or wouldn't make the needed changes and resigned. Sometimes, as they worked through the action plan and realized they weren't achieving the results, they began looking for another job, found one, and then resigned.

In my own experience, only about 10-20 percent of people who went through this process ever got to the stage where termination was necessary. Think about it. Taking people through a process that is fair and helps them avoid a termination is a blessing to them compared with what often happens in organizations.

Three Possible Outcomes

1. The problem is solved. Everyone wins in this scenario.

2. The person realizes they can't or don't want to resolve the issue and leaves with their dignity intact. This is much better for everyone than being released at the end of a 90-day or six-month timeframe.

3. The problem is not solved, and the person is released with fore-knowledge of the consequences. There is a great benefit to this. First, there is no surprise. Chances were given to improve performance. The process is fair. It is also a great protection should legal action occur later.

Corporate Example

I had just assumed responsibility for a new corporate department. The vice president in charge told me he had a member on the team who was a problem but that nothing could be done about it. He indicated there were three different sections of labor law that gave this individual protection. My view was this individual did not need protection if he was suited for the job and doing the job. But it would be unfair to the individual to leave him in the job if it wasn't a good fit. We went through the process just described. The individual saw he was not meeting the expectations of the role. He found another job outside the company that fit him better, and we did not have a lawsuit or any other repercussions from it. If we had not followed this process, I believe we would have had a very different outcome that would not have been constructive for the individual or good for the company.

103

Chapter 15

What If They Can't Do The Job?

> Is it compassionate to leave
> someone in a job they <u>can't do</u>?

The process described in the last chapter is fine when you think the person can solve the issue and they want to try. It doesn't work when the person can't do the job. Many times, I find people have been set up for failure because they simply don't have the right personality profile for the job. It may be they were hired into the job and never fit in the first place. Or, it may be that things changed within the organization and they no longer fit.

One reason managers/leaders resist making a change is that they see the situation as negative. They think, "I have to fire this person." What if you had a brain surgeon who hesitated to tell people they had brain tumors and procrastinated doing surgery? Tumors would continue to grow and likely be fatal. People who don't fit their roles for whatever reason are similar. The situation hurts them and the organization. When we think of the situation as freeing, releasing, or separating, it takes on a different dynamic.

Let's explore further by asking the question, "Can the needed results be achieved with this person in the job?" If the answer is no, the only logical thing to do is make a change. But many leaders seem very reluctant to do this. Some don't do it at all. And many do it much later than they should. In fact, many wait until they are in crisis mode and mad or upset before they take any action. This only makes the situation worse or causes them to handle it poorly—which in turn makes them more reluctant to make a timely change the next time one is needed.

A major reason we aren't willing to make personnel changes is that we view them through a paradigm we learned in organizations. Let's take a practical example. I observed a lot of hospital CEOs over many years. Some didn't appear great to me, but they had the good fortune of being in growth markets and had stellar facilities, excellent medical staffs, great leadership teams, and good labor markets. They did not build or select the teams; they were just fortunate enough to be placed there. They were given the invisible "hero" label.

Conversely, I saw some CEOs that were exceptionally smart, worked really hard, and had stellar values. They had the challenge of being in difficult markets, needing access to additional capital, having challenging medical staffs, weaker leadership teams, and an overall tougher labor market. These CEOs seldom got the "hero" label no matter how hard they worked to improve their situations.

These experiences convinced me I should throw away the invisible "hero" and "goat" labels. When I did, my whole view changed of removing people who didn't fit their roles.

Are individuals in difficult situations bad people or poor employees? Maybe it's not their fault. If they never really fit the role, it's the leader's fault for putting them in it. If a team member is undermining them, it's the team member's fault. If the culture is a barrier for them, that's the problem.

No matter how good we become at selecting people, most of us are going to make a mistake at some point. The question is: what are we going to do about it? Unless it's really bad or until it gets really bad, most leaders do nothing. After all, it's a messy job. In the traditional view, we tell ourselves we have to "fire" the person. We hate that. And

I hope we do hate it anytime it's framed that way. We feel bad for the person and about ourselves for the perceived "negative" action we're getting ready to take.

Using a more objective view, we are not saying someone in such a situation is a bad person or a bad employee.

Compassion

So here's the question—are we being kind to people when we leave them where they don't fit? Are we helping them when we leave them in a situation where they can't do the job well? The simple answer is—no. In fact, it is just plain insensitive and maybe mean.

The most compassionate thing we can do for people who don't fit their roles is to help them find places where they fit. Please notice, I said help. They have to work with us and own the responsibility for accomplishing the transition. They are more likely to cooperate wholeheartedly if we kindly, clearly, and compassionately explain to them it's better for them, better for the team, and better for the organization.

Jim got a degree from a technical school with the goal of becoming an HVAC repairman making $20 an hour. He thought this would provide a good living and all he wanted out of life at the time. His boss put his arm around him one day and said, "You're just not very good at this." He let Jim go. Jim was devastated, and I'm sure his boss felt bad. But it was the best thing that could have happened for Jim. His boss did him a favor. Jim was made to be a "dealmaker." And what a dealmaker he is! Jim has bought and sold over $2 billion worth of businesses in the past several years.

What if Jim's boss hadn't let him go? What if he had told Jim he just needed to buckle down and work harder and he would be an OK HVAC repairman? What if Jim had done that? He would have been trapped in a job that didn't use the potential God gave him. He would have become increasingly miserable in it. By the way, his personality profile pegged him as a developer, i.e., a dealmaker. Just think of the pain and misery that could have been avoided had he known this before he went to school, and if his boss had known it before hiring him. Jim was trapped in a job he didn't fit.

I'm reminded of a ministry example. A regional ministry growing to a more national scope was expanding to a new city. I saw a personality profile on a city director. I had never seen a profile like that be success-ful in that role. I asked about it. The response I got was, "We are trying to force him to grow or get out of the way."

I was appalled! I talked to the national director and asked, "Would you kick someone on crutches until they either ran or fell over?" He laughed and said, "No." I said, "Isn't that what is happening in this case?" He quickly agreed. We had a good discussion centered on the fact this was not logical. You don't kick a person on crutches and expect him to run faster. The person was boxed into a job they didn't fit. We discussed that the ministry's approach to this problem was not fair, nor was it a good spiritual way to deal with the matter. The national director agreed and stated compassionately and honestly that the person was in a role that didn't fit him anymore. Then they worked out a transition.

Chapter 16

Pitfalls in Dealing with People

> **How much more progress do you think you could make if you avoided the pitfalls of dealing with people the wrong way?**

A question I often get from leaders/managers is: how do I make people do what I want them to do? The simple answer is, you don't. The point of having cathedral builders staff your organization is that they are doing what they want to do, because they want to do it, and are happy for the opportunity. Organizations spend way too much time trying to pressure people into doing what the organization wants done without regard to what the people have talent and passion to do. If you are asking this question, you are almost guaranteed to have a lot of bricklayers in your organization.

Another issue I often get asked about is: "Things have changed, and the current team is not capable of taking us into the future. How do I put pressure on them so they leave and I can hire new team members?" The answer again is, you don't. Doing this is going to cause friction and conflict. The people in question will eventually leave, but with bad feelings toward the organization.

They may do a great deal of damage on the way out. People left in the organization that had relationships with them will think less of the organization and the leadership team. Such friction and conflict is not necessary. Why label as bad people those who have gotten you to the point you are? They're not bad people, or shouldn't be if you hired them and left them in place. If you're new to the leadership role, then someone else hired them and empowered them. That's on the person who hired them and left them in place when they were no longer a fit. Don't make it about the person in the job.

Treat them as a friend, and do them a favor that doesn't cost you anything. Share the truth with them. The organization is going in a different direction and you have concerns about whether they are going to be qualified to do the work or happy doing it. Having that discussion proactively often is appreciated and may garner acceptance and support. But under any circumstance, it is a better way to start.

Next, celebrate their years of service and contribution to the organization. Give them as much credit and esteem as you can on their way out. The remaining employees will feel better about the organization and its leadership. You will not necessarily have an enemy on the street badmouthing you and your organization. Most importantly, you will develop a reputation as an organization that people are willing to be part of. If you send your old team off in disgrace, who is going to want to step into that environment?

Remember, hire and retain people who want to do what needs to be done.

Since having the right people is a key to successful results in a successful organization, it is crucial that we get this component right. In the next graphic is a summary of pitfalls in dealing with people.

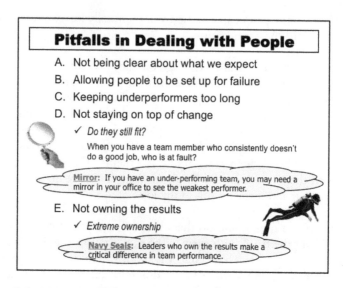

Pitfalls in Dealing with People

A. Not being clear about what we expect

B. Allowing people to be set up for failure

C. Keeping underperformers too long

D. Not staying on top of change

✓ Do they still fit?

When you have a team member who consistently doesn't do a good job, who is at fault?

Mirror: If you have an under-performing team, you may need a mirror in your office to see the weakest performer.

E. Not owning the results

✓ Extreme ownership

Navy Seals: Leaders who own the results make a critical difference in team performance.

Part of the above is self-explanatory. However, I want to speak to some of the items. We set people up for failure when we know they can't do the job but keep hoping and waiting for something to get better. This often occurs if we do not stay on top of change. Organizations tend to be dynamic. The world changes around us, and we change to adapt to the world. This has a significant impact on an organization over time. A once very productive team member may now be in a position that has outgrown them. Maybe it outgrew their skills or maybe their interests or passions. Either way, they're not happy and you aren't either.

Every year, I used to evaluate each of my direct reports. I would look at what changed and expectations for the role, their unique personality and experience, then determine if they were still a good fit going forward. I would do the same thing for myself. I asked for their input, as well as my boss's.

Finally, the key to success is the leader owning the results. If you have a consistently weak and underperforming team, the person you need to look at first and most deeply is yourself. You pick the people, train them, and create the culture and environment in which they operate. You decide who to let go and who to keep. You decide who to replace them with. Over a period of time, if you have a weak team, it's because you are a weak leader.

Chapter 17

Personality Profiles

> **How much more productive and fun could your work be if you really understood what made your people tick?**

I once accepted a meeting with a couple of men from a personality profiling company called Axiometrics International (AI). The founder was an older gentleman with flowing white hair about shoulder length. He wore a leather hat, wrinkled beige slacks, blue button-down collar shirt, and navy blue blazer with dusty brown shoes. It was two years after that initial meeting before I saw him wear anything else. His name is Wayne Carpenter. Wayne is eccentric, but brilliant. I typically refer to him as Einstein. He already knew I understood and used personality profiles in personnel selection, so he offered me a free sample of his, which I took. His profile told me things about myself I recognized as true but that had not been pointed out by any other profiling system. I was intrigued. Then he offered me two more free profiles. I had assumed responsibility for a new function about six months earlier and had a couple of people in leadership roles I thought I had figured out. But I wanted assurance.

They completed the profiles, and Wayne was able to describe these two people like he had observed their performance for years.

I thought, "How could I use this tool in hiring?" For every candidate thereafter that I interviewed who impressed me enough to go forward, I created a package which contained the candidate's résumé, a DISC personality profile, and the AI profile. Using these tools, I was able to know more about a candidate before they walked in than many leaders know after the interview. These tools helped me do a much better interview and gave me insight into delegating to them, following up, and coaching them.

Using Personality Profiles

Electricians have a lot of knowledge about wiring. In fact, they are required to have a license showing their knowledge of wiring. If they did not know what they were doing, they could electrocute themselves. They could do a faulty job and burn a building down. If this happened, other people could be hurt or killed.

Assume a building contractor allows an unlicensed electrician to work on his job. The electrician does faulty wiring, the building burns, and people are killed. What happens to the building contractor? He is sued for damages to the building. He is likely sued by family members for causing death or injury to people. It's possible he even faces criminal charges. In other words, there's great accountability for letting people deal with the wiring in the building when they don't have sufficient knowledge.

How does this apply to leadership? The height of God's creation in terms of value, worth, and complexity is human beings. Among all the resources God gives leaders to work with, the most important is people. What's more, they have unique personalities—hardwiring—that God gave them. We refer to these as personality profiles. What do most leaders understand about personality profiles in general and specifically the personality profiles of the people they are impacting? Very little! I shudder to think how little I understood about the personality profiles of people when I began leading.

Owners of businesses and leaders of other organizations often give people leadership/management responsibility with significant influence over the lives of people. These appointed managers often have very little understanding of personality profiles. When you're dealing with people "hardwired" a specific way, but you have little understanding of that hardwiring, it's likely that over time you're going to fry their minds, emotions, motivations, passions, and spirits. Fortunately, no licenses are required for leaders and managers to understand the hardwiring of their people.

God knows us intimately because He made us. Jeremiah 1:5 says, "Before I formed you in [your mother's] womb, I knew you." We can begin to understand how people are designed by understanding and using personality profiles in our work.

Have you ever seen a trout in a mountain stream? They are hard to see unless the sunlight hits them just right or they make a sudden movement. They seem to just blend in and flow with the stream. It all seems rather effortless. But not every fish fits a mountain stream so well. There are salmon that swim upstream and die after laying their eggs. Marlins don't fit a mountain stream at all. They belong in an ocean.

I remember a conversation with a guy at a key point in his career. He was trying to determine if he would take the CEO job in a big company or the CEO job in a small start-up company. After listening to him for a while, I told him he wasn't meant, at that point in his life, to be a big fish in a small pond but rather a big fish in the ocean. That statement immediately resonated with him. How God made us determines where and what we are suited for. Understanding our unique personality profile is one step toward understanding how God made us.

For purposes of this discussion, we will refer to one of the oldest and most basic personality profiles—the DISC. I use it because it is one of the easiest to understand and communicate to other people. Also, it provides a great framework for explaining the complexities of other models.

What are personality profiles?

In very simple terms, they are predictors of behavior. There are a great number of personality profiling systems available in the market. Most of them are what I call behavioral models. You answer a series of questions and, based on your answers, they predict your behavioral patterns.

Why do I use them?

The simple reason is because of the experience I explained at the beginning of this chapter. Using personality profiles does not guarantee you will be able to predict people's behavior and performance 100 percent of the time. In fact, there are two key mistakes you could make. One is not using profiles as a tool, and the other is relying on them so much that you don't cover all aspects of an effective interview process. Using the profile has increased my success rate in hiring effective employees. It's also helped me in knowing what I can delegate to a person, how to influence their motivation, and what coaching will take them to the next level.

What I use

I use two different profiling systems. One is TTI Success Insights, which produces a traditional DISC profile that I will explain later. The DISC system is a very basic profile that's been around for many years. It is inexpensive and easier to use and understand than the more complicated system.

I also use AI. This system is what I refer to as a mental model. It evaluates how you think, see the world internally and externally, and make decisions. The DISC profile is one that can be easily manipulated if you've ever taken one before. By contrast, the AI cannot be manipulated, but you can get a false result if the instructions are not properly followed.

114

How I use them

First, I find a résumé with which I'm sufficiently impressed to bring the person in for an interview. Then I ask them to complete the two profiles. Each one takes approximately 20 to 30 minutes to complete, so the process is not onerous. Since the DISC can be manipulated and the AI can yield a false reading if the instructions are not properly followed, I compare the two to see if they make contradictory assessments. If they do, I talk to the candidate in an attempt to determine which one is incorrect and usually allow the candidate to retake one or both of them.

Then I compare the results of the profiles to the résumé to see if their hardwiring matches up with the work responsibilities and results I see on the résumé. I then use all of this information to prepare for the interview.

In a typical interview, I know more about the person coming in than many people know about a candidate after the interview is over. Based on what I see on the résumé and in the personality profile, I am able to ask a series of targeted questions related to the uniqueness of that individual rather than conducting a general all-purpose interview. I do ask enough questions to validate what I see in the personality profiles as I discuss the résumé. Finally, I make a decision.

Once a person is hired using this process, I have a much better understanding of their strengths and weaknesses. That helps in assignment, teamwork, and coaching for that individual.

How does it work?

In the DISC system:

The "D" stands for <u>dominant</u>. *These people are driven to get results.*

The "I" stands for <u>influencer</u>. *These people are very social. They tend to be the life of the party. They never meet a stranger.*

The "S" stands for <u>steady</u>. *These people tend to stay calm when others panic. They are very team oriented.*

The **"C" stands for <u>competent</u>.** *These people are analytical, intuitive, and very detail oriented. The chart on the next page gives more details about the characteristics of each.*

DISC

C = Competent
- Conscientious authority
- Analytical
- Sensitive
- Factual
- Diplomatic

D = Dominant
- Driving achiever
- Makes quick decisions
- Takes action
- Forceful
- Time conscious

S = Steady
- Steady worker
- Loyal
- Patient
- Specialist
- Team member

I = Influencing
- Influential personality
- Helpful
- Persuasive
- Emotional
- Trusting

See the appendix for more explanation on how these tools are used in the work environment.

People Section Questions

1. Do you have the right team to achieve the organization's vision?

2. If some people no longer fit their roles, what are you doing about it?

3. Do you treat people with respect if you have to move them out of your organization?

4. Do you believe everybody wins when people are in roles that fit them best? Do you use personality profile tools to achieve this?

PROGRESS
INTRODUCTION

Everyone has a basic need to make progress. People can go to a 4-year-old T-ball game where they don't keep score. Yet all the adults walk out knowing the score. People wouldn't play golf or watch sports if there were no score.

Progress doesn't just happen. It takes effort and a plan. I've always been a planner by nature. I grew up on a family farm in western Kentucky. I'm grateful for what the experience taught me. Yet I did not plan to live on a farm all my life. So I planned to go to college.

I planned many things in college, one of which was my dating life. Time passes fast. All of the sudden, I realized I was a junior and would not have the same opportunities in a couple of years. So the first semester of my junior year, I decided to date many different girls. I had dates with different girls every weekend.

That sounds successful. But it wasn't. I found myself asking out nice, smart, attractive girls that I thought would go out with me, but not the ones I most wanted to date. I got to my senior year and had a different plan. I decided to go for it. I created what I called my chicken list. This was the list of girls I most wanted to date during college but didn't have the guts to ask out. If someone turned me down, I would not see them after the next year anyway. I started methodically down that list.

118

Some already had dates when I called. Others were busy with other commitments, or so they said. Some just turned me down, though they were nice about it.

The girl at the top of my list always seemed to be out of her room. She had not turned me down. I just couldn't get in touch with her. I always got no answer or talked to her roommate. I found out later she had me confused with some other country boy, and she didn't want to take his call.

I determined to make one final call and as providence would have it, she answered. I asked her out. She quickly accepted. Five months later, I gave her a ring and asked her to marry me. Nine months later, we were married. That was 42 years ago.

The point is, to achieve a goal you have to have a plan. My plan started with a written list and methodical persistence until I failed or reached the goal. I married the girl at the top of my list! I learned by experience that it's better to set a high goal and miss it than to set a low one and hit it. The rest of my life, I set goals many people said couldn't be met. Most of them were!

> At this point, you may be thinking, "The reason I read this book on leadership is to make progress. Why did you wait until the last section to start talking about progress?" Let's think about that for minute.
>
> - If your purpose or mission is not clear, what are you going to make progress toward?
> - If you do not have clear and unchanging priorities, how will you determine the path to progress?
> - If you don't have the right people in place, who will help you make progress?
> - If you don't empower people properly, how will they contribute to the progress?

119

In other words, the other topics covered first are foundational to making progress. I have found there are six keys to helping an organization make progress:

1. Planning

2. Avoiding mistakes

3. Leading change projects

4. Creating documentation and training

5. Establishing enabling control systems

6. Establishing high-impact measures and sharing results with your team

---

The Bottom Line

- Progress requires a plan, a control system, good documentation and training, measurements, and feedback.

- Leaders enable progress, share results, and celebrate success while managers direct and control projects.

- Leaders position teams for progress while managers simply reach objectives.

Chapter 18

Nehemiah's Plan

> **Desiring progress without a plan
> is an empty wish or dream.**

I have made many plans since having success on my college "chicken list." You may ask, "What does a good plan look like?" There's probably no better model for planning than the one we see in the Old Testament book of Nehemiah. See below a schematic of his planning process.

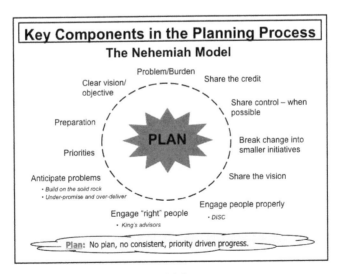

Key Components in the Planning Process

The Nehemiah Model

Problem/Burden

Clear vision/ objective

Share the credit

Share control – when possible

Preparation

PLAN

Break change into smaller initiatives

Priorities

Anticipate problems
· Build on the solid rock
· Under-promise and over-deliver

Share the vision

Engage people properly
· DISC

Engage "right" people
· King's advisors

Plan: No plan, no consistent, priority driven progress.

Problem/opportunity. Nehemiah's planning process started with a burden or problem and an opportunity.

> *"They said to me,*
> *'The remnant there in the providence*
> *who survived captivity are in great distress and*
> *reproach, and the wall of Jerusalem was broken*
> *down and its gates are burned with fire.'"*
> *Nehemiah 1:3*

The passion in people rises when something makes them mad, glad, or sad. We are glad when we see a great opportunity and thus begin planning to capitalize on it. In Nehemiah's case, he was sad, and God revealed to him an opportunity to do something about the situation.

Prayer. Nehemiah 1:4-6 says he "sat down and wept and mourned for days; and was fasting and praying before the God of heaven." In his prayer time, Nehemiah got perfectly aligned with God. He confessed his own sins and those of his people. Then he was prepared to hear God's plan for him. Regardless of religious affiliation or spiritual background, most people pray. Usually, it's not if they pray; it's simply when and how they pray. Most people tend to get in a jam following their own plans and then begin asking God to help them out. There is a reason the Proverbs say, "and lean not on your own understanding."

Some people make up their minds and then pray for God to bless their plans. That's not how Nehemiah prayed. He had a burden after hearing what happened to his home city of Jerusalem and took his burden before the Lord.

Prayer is where God reveals His plan to us. We like to talk about vision in organizational life. For the Christian, vision is really God's revelation of His plan and of our involvement. Nehemiah had a vision for rebuilding the wall in Jerusalem. But that came from God, and Nehemiah was to have a leadership role in it. He was clear about God's vision and his role in it before he did anything else. He was to go and rebuild the wall. He knew this was going to take an incredible amount of work.

Preparation. Nehemiah thought and made preparations for what would be required next and for the questions that would be asked of him. More prayer was part of his preparation. In Nehemiah 1:11, he prayed that God would give the king compassion to help him. Let's not take lightly the prayer time of Nehemiah as he prepared. People who served the king in that day and were sad in the king's presence were subject to dismissal from their role or even death. Nehemiah prayed for the king's favor and showed his sadness in Nehemiah 2: "Now I had not been sad in his presence. So he said to me, 'Why is your face sad though you are not sick? This is nothing but sadness of heart.'" Nehemiah told him why. The king said to him, "What would you request?" This is where preparation in prayer and good administrative thinking came in. Nehemiah said, "If it please the King, and if your servant has found favor before you, send me to Judah, to the city of my father's tombs, that I may rebuild it." Next is where his administrative thinking in advance came into play. The king asked, "How long will your journey be, and when will you return?" So it pleased the king to send him, and he gave the king a definite timeframe for the project. There was a lot involved in rebuilding the walls of Jerusalem. Nehemiah must have spent hours thinking and figuring how long this massive endeavor would take. Therefore, when asked, he had a sure and ready answer.

I have seen leaders make many mistakes in this area over the years. I made my share as well. The first mistake is not being able to answer basic questions about the cost and timeline when you're asking permission to do a big project. Another mistake is under-resourcing a project. There is a tendency to want to lowball the cost and time required to increase the chances of getting approval for a project. This usually comes back to bite you when you have to go back and ask for more resources. It's harder to get them after you miss your initial estimates and don't live up to your commitments than it is to request more in the beginning.

Perhaps the biggest mistake people make in organizational life is the tendency to systemically overpromise and under-deliver. We had an initiative in Physician Services once, which we started small and spread through several hospitals and divisions. The concept had been sufficiently tested and proven, so we asked the CEO for funding to expand the initiative. We had worked for weeks on the business plan, and the team anticipated a $200 million measurable benefit over five years to the company. I looked at the business plans and thought the results were achievable if everything went right, but there was not much margin for error, and some of the results were based on what I considered soft measures. I asked the team to cut the measurable benefit in the projections to $100 million. The team asked me why. I said, "Let's think through this. If we promise $200 million in benefits and deliver $150 million, are you going to get an 'attaboy!' for the $150 million or be criticized for the $50 million miss? By contrast, if we promise a $100 million benefit and deliver $150 million in benefit, how do you think that will be received? Which position would you prefer to be in?" The team got the point and quickly agreed to make the changes.

The discussion didn't end there though. I explained there was more to my thinking. If I let the discussion stop there, they might have thought the goal on an initiative is to "sandbag" the results. That wasn't my intent at all. I brought up several potential barriers to the $200 million projection and asked if we had contingency plans to fill gaps. I asked if anybody thought the soft numbers in the projections would be attacked by some senior executives in the boardroom when we went for approval. Scripture tells us to "build on the solid rock" (Matthew 7:24-27). I know scripture is talking about building something solid spiritually. But I do think there is a practical application of that spiritual principle. Build on what is solid.

Many times I've seen people go to meetings with seven justifications for a project. The first four are rock solid and what I call "no-brainers." The last three are potential benefits but more questionable, with the last one being a bit of a stretch. The presenters should have gone for the easy win, stating the four concrete justifications and stopping at that for approval. Instead though, they presented all seven justifications, and projects were not approved or were delayed because of ensuing discussion over the less concrete benefits. I counseled the team to build on what was rock solid so we did not risk losing credibility over things that could be seen by others as a bit of a stretch, even if we believed we were right.

Scripture speaks of "going the extra mile." With this phrase, Jesus taught people to do more than they were required by law to do. An extension of this principle is doing more than you promised to do. People who systemically overpromise and under-deliver are not seen as trustworthy, even though they may deliver substantial results over time.

When we got to the boardroom with this initiative, the team was well prepared, and it went pretty much as we had anticipated. After substantial discussion with people trying unsuccessfully to poke holes in the projections, the company CEO asked a question. He turned, looked me straight in the eye, and said, "Leon, how sure are you about this $100 million in benefits?" Because the team had prepared so well and left in the projections only what we knew was solid, I was able to look him in the eye and say, "I have a 95 percent confidence level in that number and the fact it is likely conservative. How many times in the past have I told you we could do something that we didn't deliver on or exceed?" He said, "$100 million over five years is enough for me. Does anybody else have any questions?" Of course, there were none, and our initiative was approved.

Establish priorities. Any good plan must have clear priorities. In Nehemiah 2, Nehemiah went out at night and inspected the wall. What was he doing? He was continuing his thinking and preparation process. Now he was thinking about priorities.

Anticipate obstacles. Nehemiah did this, but many leaders overlook it. Nehemiah 2:7-8 states, "And I said to the King, 'If it please the King, let letters be given me for the governors of the provinces beyond the river, that they may allow me to pass through until I come to Judah, and a letter to Asaph, the keeper of the King's forest, that he may give me timber to make beams for the gates of the fortress which is by the Temple, for the wall of the city and for the house to which I will go.'" Often, leaders make plans and do not anticipate issues that can arise from their decisions. Thus, they wind up spending enormous amounts of time solving problems that could have been anticipated and solved with preemptive planning.

Engage the right people. Nehemiah only took a few men with him to inspect the walls. He said, "I did not tell anyone what God was putting into my mind to do for Jerusalem" (Nehemiah 2:12). He apparently only took a few men who were most trustworthy and could help the most in planning this massive project. Engaging the right people is critical for any leader. When Jethro was advising Moses to engage other leaders and share the load with them, he advised Moses to find trustworthy leaders and he explained what that entailed (Exodus 18:21). In 1 Kings 12:6, youthful King Rehoboam consulted two groups of people. He asked the elders, who had served his father Solomon, what to do. They said, "If you will be a servant to this people today, and will serve them and grant them their petition, and speak good words to them, then they will be your servant forever." Sadly for him, he did not listen to their counsel. Instead, he went to the young men who grew up with him. They advised him to make life harder for people and to show his leadership by abusive strength rather than service or kindness. Rehoboam took that advice. Because of his harsh response to people, most of them quit following him and rejected him as king. Engaging the right people and listening to them is a key characteristic of any successful leader.

Engage people properly. People's personality profiles are a huge driver of what they contribute to the team and how to properly engage them. You may recall our discussion about how to engage the various personality profiles.

- **The dominant personalities** are going to speak quickly, make decisions quickly, and want to take control. Once a project is well planned, it's fine for them to be the project coordinator.

- **The influencer personalities** are going to speak quickly and often and are willing to promote the project and care for the people aspects of the initiative.

- **The steady personalities** are going to be responsible for doing much of the work. They know how to do the work and are great team members. They do not speak up as quickly. Therefore, you must create a comfortable forum for their input or ask for it directly and encourage them to share their perspective.

- **The complaint or cautious personalities** are going to think of detailed questions to ask and issues that could arise that nobody else is thinking about. They also are generally going to be hesitant to speak up. But it's crucial that their insights be sought and listened to. A great number of mistakes can be avoided by listening to these people. Also, oftentimes they are able to improve already good ideas.

Leaders without training or perspective on the unique personality profiles of their team are going to have difficulty engaging people the right way.

Share the vision. In Nehemiah 2:18, we see the response of the people as they say, "Let us arise and build." This vision was not something Nehemiah dreamed up on his own. God put it in his heart. Nehemiah articulated the vision and encouraged the people. And he did it in a way that inspired them so that it became a shared vision, reflected by their statement, "Let us arise and build." Many leaders ride into town like a new sheriff, calling attention to themselves, assigning blame and criticizing others, barking out orders, and expecting compliance. That was not Nehemiah's way at all. He came as a servant.

He did not demand any of the rights he had as governor, and he shared the vision with the people so that they owned it and were excited about it.

Break change into smaller initiatives. Nehemiah broke the work into small initiatives that could be shared with people.

Share the work. Nehemiah led the work, but people did the work. Notice that people did the work for which they volunteered and most wanted to do. Nehemiah was a very astute leader. Nehemiah 3 reveals that most people rebuilt the wall in front of their house. When Nehemiah let people rebuild the wall in front of their house, they were doing the portion of the work that they cared about, and they did it with great care and enthusiasm.

Share control when possible. People like to take charge of their own destiny. Sometimes, however, there is a crisis situation and the leader has to take strong control to get through it. When the building is on fire, it's time for someone to take charge, not call a committee meeting.

Share the credit. Unlike many leaders, when the project was completed, Nehemiah called a meeting and shared the credit with everyone. He did not brag or call attention to himself in any way. He objectively stated what each group had done to achieve the great feat. Then he turned the ceremony over to the priests so they could lead the celebration. Everything he did was to shine the spotlight on others and not draw attention to himself.

Chapter 19

Levels of Planning

**Does your detailed planning include
the individual level or just the
higher levels of planning?**

We will talk about the various levels of planning in this chapter so you
can understand how to go from very high-level plans to specific, individual goals. This process is what I call cascading priorities through the
organization. There are several levels of planning in an organization:

Levels of Planning

✓ Visionary objectives

✓ Strategic initiatives

✓ Annual goals

- Total Organization
- Operating Units
- Corporate Departments
- Individuals

✓ Action plans/project management

You start at the top of the organization with a broad vision and set of objectives and cascade those through the organization to individuals and specific actions. See below a set of visional five-year objectives for an example nonprofit organization.

Visionary Objectives (example)

We are a premiere organization that:

- Is the first place ministry partners go for help in achieving their mission

- Develops cutting-edge training programs for partners

- Leverages technology to expand and improve services while reducing costs

- Shares organizational knowledge to help others achieve a similar level of excellence

---

The visionary objectives are translated into measurable goals for the organization for that year. In the example above, the broad objectives are for a nonprofit organization. Each year, businesses usually set concrete dollar metrics or percentage increases as their goals, like the next example.

Sample Business Goals – Short Form

	Goal	YTD Actual
1.	Increase existing mid-level contribution to fixed overhead/profits by $120,000	
2.	Increase aesthetics profits by 10% (approx. $80K revenue impact and $40K profit impact)	
3.	Lower overhead as a percent of gross profit by 2% (approx. $85-$100K+ impact)	

Setting goals in business organizations is usually pretty straightforward. You are trying to hit a measurable target by a specific time.

It gets a bit more difficult sometimes in nonprofits and ministries. They don't always lend themselves to the same exacting measures as a business. With nonprofits and ministries, I use what I call the long form to goal setting. I also use this form a lot in corporate support functions for businesses.

Sample Long Form Ministry Goals

	Goal	Standard	Year to Date
1.	Resource partners in the area of stewardship to advance our work.	• Achieve 7.5% giving average by December 2019 • Raise $1 million through special offerings by 12/31/18	
2.	Create online training for partners and other ministry leaders.	• One hundred leaders will have completed 100 hours on online training by 12/31/19 • Formal and informal surveys validate that at least 75% of participants believe the training will make a meaningful difference in their ministry and they will be able to give examples of such. • At least 50% of participants will show a desire for additional training and would recommend a friend receive some of the training.	

First, I determine the goal. What are we trying to improve or achieve? Then I ask the team what success looks like for the goal. We answer that question by establishing measurable standards. In the example above, goal number one is easily measured by specific percentages or dollars, just like in a business. Goal number two is more challenging. Coming up with the number of leaders to complete the training by specific time is easy. Determining how we're going to assess the quality of the training is more difficult. The best way to achieve an objective standard in this case is to survey participants about how valuable the training was.

Notice also the year to date column on the forms. This is for the quarterly report we will discuss later.

Chapter 20

Stop the Mistakes!

How much could you accomplish if you weren't "putting out fires" all the time?

A lot of problems are created in our planning processes because of unintended consequences. My Internal Audit experience taught me the importance of anticipating and trying to eliminate problems. I learned that good control systems are proactive and offer early warnings so that more substantial problems are anticipated. Making progress in organizations is like making money in your investment portfolio. The first rule is: preserve capital. The second rule is: preserve capital. And the third rule is: don't forget rules one and two. Stated more plainly, the first rule of making money is to not lose money. Don't go backwards.

You will never make it to the top of the mountain if you keep stumbling and falling back down.

In organizations, progress is like climbing a mountain. You can only get to the top if you don't stumble and fall to the bottom. It reminds me of professional sports. Here's the question for you sports fans: How many professional games are won rather than lost? Here is what I mean. Sometimes, a team goes on the field and plays a superior game, defeating an able opponent. They win. Yet frequently games are decided by one team committing more fatal errors than the other. In football, excessive penalties cause the loss of games. Sometimes the penalties aren't even close to the ball and are completely unnecessary. Sometimes it's a dropped pass that hits the receiver in the chest. Sometimes, it's a missed tackle. Sometimes, it's a missed field goal.

My point is, I've seen more professional football games lost due to fundamental errors than I have seen won due to superior playing.

**Basic errors often
cause teams to lose.**

I see the same thing in basketball. I've seen national championship games lost because of a very low shooting percentage from the free-throw line. Games sometimes are decided by missed layups, unnecessary fouls, or technical fouls due to flaring tempers.

You may say, "What does this have to do with organizations?" Everything! I see the same thing in businesses and other organizations. Mistakes stop progress. Frequently, the mistakes in organizations stem from our overinflated egos. Our goals seem to be oriented toward hitting a homerun, the grand slam, rather than consistently hitting singles and not committing errors. The homeruns are flashier, but trying to hit them tends to yield a lot of strikeouts and other mistakes. Singles aren't glamorous, but a team that aims for singles generally makes fewer mistakes and, in turn, wins games. How many times have we seen large, well-established businesses go bankrupt because of substantial errors? Their business models were not flawed. Their employees were good and talented. But someone, usually the leadership, made a mistake that took the company down.

> **Everyone hitting a single is going to win nearly every game. Occasionally, you may win because of a "grand slam."**

The first key to getting ahead is: don't go backward. Avoiding errors, anticipating unintended consequences, and being proactive are the keys to not going backward.

I dealt with a handful of turnaround situations in my career. I called these "firefighting" situations. The organizations spent so much time dealing with problems and learning not to make mistakes. The people worked extremely hard but couldn't make any progress. The natural tendency of leaders is just to work harder to put out the fires and try to eke out some progress. My approach was to triage the fires.

> **It's hard to get ahead in organizational life when you're fighting fires all the time.**

Metaphorically speaking, I first determined if it was a gas fire, wood fire, or brush fire. Gas fires cannot be put out by pouring water on them. Organizationally, these are the types of fires that don't go away with just more time and energy. They arise from systemic problems and must be extinguished by eliminating the source, just like a gas fire has to be put out by cutting off the gas. This is one of the most important things a leader can do in a turnaround situation—identifying and stopping systemic problems.

Next, I identified the wood burning fires. These fires are very hot and will "burn the house down." They are worth the time and energy to put out in an organization and are a high priority.

The brush fires will burn themselves out without much damage if left alone. There are some problems in an organization that are isolated and will go away if left alone.

When I went into turnaround situations, I used a consistent approach. First, I distinguished between the small fires and the big fires. When you focus on priorities, you realize some small fires will burn out, but the big fires will "burn the house down." I also learned some small fires will become big fires and "burn the house down." So focus on root issues and take action on things that could cause big fires. Generally, it takes far less time to anticipate a problem than it does to fix a problem. Also, a lot of the problems in organizations are systemic. If you don't get to the root cause, they will happen repeatedly, consuming enormous time. My experience as an internal auditor taught me to look for systemic problems rather than isolated ones.

Fixing the root cause of big problems is the first step to freeing up a lot of time in a "firefighting" organization. Then, take time and put out the smaller fires with potential to become really big fires—wood burning fires. That saves another big block of time down the road. Understand that in the meantime, some of the smaller fires will have burned out by themselves—brush fires.

After the fires are extinguished, you can use firefighting time to move the organization forward.

Many otherwise good leaders significantly underestimate the importance of anticipating outcomes and avoiding unintended consequences. Look at the big oil company British Petroleum (BP). A problem that never should have occurred and would have cost very little to have avoided cost the company billions of dollars. Or look at Exxon with the Valdez spill. This was a completely avoidable problem that cost the organization billions of dollars to solve.

So much focus is put on moving ahead that sometimes little attention is paid to things that will move us backward. Let's think about some practical areas where we overlook opportunities to anticipate problems.

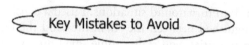

Key Mistakes to Avoid

Alignment of the goals among individuals and departments/functions in the organization is key to progress. When the organization has one set of goals and the individuals have different goals, what happens? The individual goals win out in the short-term and may hurt the organization.

Individuals pursuing their own goals is not something that should surprise leaders. Following our human nature, we are inherently self-focused.

Even among facilities owned by the same company, there is often competition rather than cooperation. I remember a hospital system that owned several hospitals in a major market. One of the hospitals had 90 percent of the obstetrics (OB) market share. Another hospital nearby decided this was a good, profitable business. They decided to convert existing space and started an OB program. After some time, the first hospital had 50 percent of the market share. The second hospital had 40 percent market share. The problem is both facilities were owned by the same organization. It had the same 90-percent market share as before, but had overhead in two facilities competing for the same patients. In large organizations with multiple units, it takes good planning to align objectives so entities cooperate rather than compete with one another.

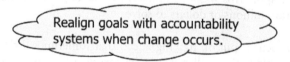

Realign goals with accountability systems when change occurs.

It is easy, especially in large organizations, to set up financial incentive systems and be too slow to change them as the environment changes. In the healthcare system, the ability to measure quality of care at hospitals began changing, as did the payment mechanisms to incentivize quality care. A particular system had many incentives for their leaders based only on the year's financial results. In meetings and speeches, the CEO kept focusing on quality results. Professionals were hired to help improve quality of care. But things seemed to change very little. Marked improvement in quality of care came only when the organization changed its financial incentives to factor in improvement in quality scores at hospitals.

Chapter 21

Leading Change

> **What potential are you forfeiting by not being proactive in leading change?**

Let me tell you how <u>not</u> to lead change. Early in my career, I had just assumed leadership responsibilities for the Internal Audit Department at HCA. The culture, the processes, and the results all needed to change. The department needed to gain more credibility, and that needed to happen within a year. I locked myself away in my office for a few days, including some weekend time. I came up with goals I saw as critical to what we needed to accomplish in the next year.

I called a meeting of my direct reports and proudly laid out the goals and initiatives we would need to accomplish. I waited for my team to respond, expecting them to be impressed with the thoroughness of my work and the soundness of my plans, and to appreciate the fact I figured all this out for the team without making them do it. It seems so foolish now, but I was genuinely surprised at their near rebellion. It wasn't that they didn't think the plans were good; they were simply overwhelmed by them. Being a new leader, I did the only thing I could think of. I retreated!

138

I asked them what they thought were the most important changes we needed to make. They told me. I asked them what we could get done in the next month. We wrote it down and agreed. I asked which of the proposed changes we could make in the next week. We wrote those down and agreed. We did this every week for a month. At the end of the month, we had accomplished more than we thought we could do that first month.

We went through the process for another month. We made plans weekly and monitored progress. At the end of the second month, we had accomplished more than we had targeted for the month.

Now I could see the team was gaining momentum. So we tried the same process again, but this time we set goals for the next three months. We monitored progress monthly. At the end of three months, we had exceeded the goals we set. We continued to do this for the balance of the year. At the end of the year, we had accomplished more than the goals and initiatives I outlined initially.

Dick Wells, author of *16 Stones*,[9] says the difference between your present position and your vision is the change necessary to achieve your desired future. We all deal with change in organizational life. In my experience, the initial reaction to change is either skepticism or outright resistance unless people are already clamoring for change. Some leaders avoid making changes until they absolutely have to because of some people's tendency not to like change. Your "S" personalities don't tend to like change, though "D" personalities thrive on it.

Successful Change

Nehemiah provides an example of change led successfully. Scripture teaches the same principles I learned by experience in my change initiatives.

Involve the Team. People like to have a say in change that affects them. We all know that from experience. They're much more accepting of change they help plan. Nehemiah was masterful at involving people in change (see Nehemiah 2:17-18). When people have input about plans and deadlines, they feel ownership and commitment that don't exist when plans are simply announced. Plus, you usually avoid a lot of unintended consequences and get better ideas by having everyone involved. Remember, the "S" and "C" temperaments see unintended consequences the "D" and "I" temperaments don't.

We can take a cue from Jesus. He wants to change our lives and change them radically. Yet in Revelation 3:20 we read, "Behold I stand at the door and knock. If anyone hears my voice and opens the door, I will come in." Think about this. If the creator of our universe waits for an invitation to come in and change us, shouldn't we think long and hard about forcing people to change? It's much better to invite and lead change than to force it.

Set goals the team believes are achievable–start small. In my earlier example, the team was overwhelmed with the goals I laid out for the year. By contrast, Nehemiah only asked the people to build the wall six inches per day. Time proved that my plans were achievable because we accomplished even more. But my plans were more than the team could absorb initially. People's experiences and personality profiles determine the timeframes in which changes need to be accomplished.

Control The Pace. Some personalities can get overwhelmed. Others tend to set goals too high. Some leaders, knowing people tend to fight change, assume the best way to make it is to force it and get it over with. That does work sometimes, but you always pay a price for it, and it's very risky. You don't know how people will respond. Sometimes a forced change is the "straw that breaks the camel's back." People in the organization may have already accumulated a lot of baggage and pent up emotions.

Starting small and controlling the pace allows us to do pilot testing before making a larger commitment. Also, starting small tends to generate less pushback from people comfortable with the status quo. We observe businesses doing this all the time. HCA piloted new computer software before largescale rollouts. Restaurants pilot new menus in key markets before making nationwide changes. Starting small and controlling the pace has key benefits.

When team members respond negatively to a perceived threat caused by change, it's wise to sit with them quickly and try to understand what else is going on in their lives. Most of the time, I found their behavior or attitude was driven by something going on in their lives other than work circumstances. By understanding that, we could avoid damaged relationships and problems in our organization downstream.

Share the credit. After the wall-building project was completed, Nehemiah called a great gathering of the people (Nehemiah 8). Yet unlike many leaders who would call such a gathering and take credit for the success, perhaps sharing some credit with their key leaders, Nehemiah brought no attention to himself at all. Rather, he put the priests in charge of the event. They celebrated success. Nehemiah acknowledged the work of every group of people. He didn't brag on the top performers. He acknowledged the amount of work they all did, and he didn't criticize the ones who did the least. Rather, he acknowledged what they did to contribute to the success of the whole project. Nehemiah didn't take any of the credit. He didn't seek the approval or accolades of the people. He only asked for one thing. He asked God to remember his service and sacrifice.

Benefits

I have seen change done poorly with significant negative results for organizations. I've seen good churches have a mass exodus because of change led poorly. Yet change led in proper ways has four major benefits.

Reduces Pushback

Incremental change yields less resistance. If I had a 300-page book and asked people to read it, many would feel overwhelmed. They would explain how busy they were and how it would be nearly impossible for them to read the book with everything else going on. If I gave them the same book and asked if they could take 10 minutes and read 10 pages that day or evening, most people would say yes. If I did that for 30 days, they would have read the 300-page book. I have actually used that approach to get feedback on this book. I have asked people to read a section at a time and give feedback rather than read the whole book at once.

Often, people procrastinate because they feel overwhelmed at the size of the project. That's why it is so important to break big projects into small pieces.

Remember my example earlier of leading changes at the audit team? When the team worked together to break big initiatives into small projects, there was no pushback against moving forward.

The TV industry has used a gradual approach to impact our culture and society significantly, though not in a positive way. When I had children and started watching reruns of programs from when I was a kid, I was struck by the changes in language, violence, sexual innuendos, and values over 30 years. If the programming we watched today had been aired 30 years ago in this nation, there would have been a rebellion, and families would have turned off their TVs. But because the change in content occurred gradually, it never reached the tipping point where people rebelled and quit watching.

Improves Cost and Efficiency

This principle works in computer conversions. After computer software is changed, it is implemented in a pilot. It stays in the pilot until all the bugs are worked out. It saves considerable time and cost to pilot new software rather than immediately implement it on a broad scale. Imagine the time and costs required to fix computer bugs at multiple locations across a large organization. HCA went through a major computer conversion one time, involving over 300 hospitals we operated. We went through the process of pilot testing the new system and made numerous modifications. Imagine the time, cost, and disruption to operations and the resistance to change if we had implemented the new software in 300 facilities without first doing a pilot in one. Pilot projects are designed so that they are not overwhelming.

Starting small with pilot testing increases efficiency over the long run because problems are avoided. When national restaurant chains want to change their menus, what do they do? They take one restaurant or market and pilot the change. They see reaction to the change. They make any needed modifications and retest. Then they begin to roll out the new items to all their restaurants. If the change is not successful, they haven't failed in 3,000 restaurants. They've failed in one restaurant or in one market. Any changes needed are made in the pilot and not in 3,000 restaurants.

Decreases Risk of Failure

Many times at HCA, starting small decreased the risk of failure. The best example is computer conversions. A change in software was not distributed across 150 hospitals at once. Instead there was an alpha pilot, which was one hospital. Bugs were worked out of the system in the pilot site before further distribution. Imagine the time and cost to correct program bugs across an entire system of hospitals. The angst created by this could cause an otherwise successful conversion to be shut down because of widespread disruption.

Creates Multiple Celebrations

One thing my personality profile guru told me about myself is that I tend to go from one goal to the next without taking time to celebrate and appreciate the contribution of the team. I have to plead guilty. Just today, I advised a young contractor to plan celebrations like he would plan anything else on a job checklist and count them as part of the job. When you break work into smaller pieces, you have more opportunities to celebrate success as you go. This encourages and strengthens the team.

Complex Change / Big Organization

When I led HCA's Physician Services Department, we initiated a hospital-based anesthesia initiative by working with a division president. I believed we were paying too much in anesthesia subsidies because we did not have enough expertise at the local level in many situations. We found an individual who was very qualified, but we couldn't get approval to put that individual on the payroll. I talked to one division president who was always good to work with and had a big opportunity in this area. I asked if he would do a pilot where we paid this person to do anesthesia contracting and negotiation as a consultant. I said-Physician Services would pay half if his division would pay half. We had enough room in the budget for the consulting fee, but couldn't get approval for an added person on the payroll.

We ran the pilot for six months and saved so much money in anesthesia subsidies that we were able to get approval to hire the person fulltime. We did a lot of work, and that division showed substantial results. Then we expanded the initiative to other divisions within that group with great success. Over three years, we developed an extensive team and did work throughout the company with many millions of dollars in savings. Without a creative, low-risk approach, this initiative would not have gotten started.

Over 12 years, we added a number of service lines and major initiatives within the Physician Services function. They all had national influence, but each was started as a pilot and implemented throughout the company gradually. Not a single one could have been sold as a national initiative from the beginning.

Another key to implementing complex change was giving others the credit at every opportunity. We were most effective when pointing to an operational success in which we took part rather than trying to take credit for an initiative. After a successful pilot, we would point to operations and give them all the credit. When I say give them all the credit, I really mean give it all. Ultimately, they were the ones responsible for executing the initiative, and it wouldn't have been needed without them. People have a tendency to take some of the credit because they want to be recognized for their contributions. Yet there is a biblical principle people either don't know or don't follow. Scripture says give freely and it will be given to you, pressed down and running over. I have seen this promise played out over and over again. The more I insist on giving others credit, the more comfortable they are in giving it back. It's not a game you play, but it is a principal absolutely worth living by.

> *"Do not claim honor in the presence of the King,*
> *and do not stand in the place of great men."*
> *Proverbs 25:6*

Our role in the process was always revealed ultimately, and we were given the opportunity to help the next set of operators. Small pilots became very large initiatives over time using this approach.

Wrong! Idea of the Week Leaders

Some leaders see themselves as change agents when, in fact, they are simply "idea of the week" leaders. Most organizations of any size have one somewhere. Change for the sake of change without a clear plan and use of pilots to monitor success is not the way to implement change.

Some leaders say the process or people are not working out, and they begin making changes without the counsel of others and without a plan. This often results in no improvement or in the situation getting worse. Too much change, change not well planned, or change in which the team has not been involved usually yields poor results.

Entrepreneurial leaders in for-profit and nonprofit organizations tend to implement change improperly a lot. They are often creative by nature, get bored easily, and make changes for the sake of change. There are certain personality profiles that are highly creative and have problems with the status quo. Sometimes they make unnecessary changes. There is a difference between leaders who promote continual change programs toward a "vision" and creative leaders who are "idea of the week" or "idea of the month" leaders.

Chapter 22

Progress Through Documentation and Training

> **How much time could you save if what you knew was well documented and people were trained?**

Dr. Frist, Sr. used to say mankind started making its most significant progress after we learned to write. In fact, there was a significant change among mankind after the invention of the printing press. Being able to document what we have learned so each generation doesn't have to reinvent the wheel has been significant to our progress.

We see the same thing in organizations. When I led the Internal Audit Department, we dealt with turnover. Even though it improved, turnover was still high in our department compared to other corporate functions. That was the nature of the Internal Audit Department because it was used as a training ground and promotion opportunity for many

146

professionals. As we tried to add value to the company through our work, I began to hire specialists in certain areas. They would do great work and take our capabilities to new levels.

They would normally stay about two years before someone else in the company hired them because of their specialized knowledge. Then it felt like we would start all over again with someone new.

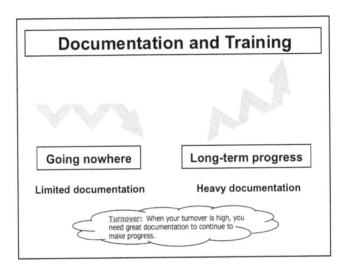

Then, I committed that we would create heavy documentation of everything our specialists knew. We created detailed audit programs. We added supplements to the audit programs that explained in detail the thought process and best methods for completing each step. We designed preprinted work papers to facilitate consistent gathering of information. Once we did this, we did not lose all the expertise of a person that moved somewhere else in the company. In fact, the replacement was able to get up to speed very quickly and usually improved on what we already had developed.

Following this protocol helped us avoid peaks and valleys in the quality of our work. Over time, our expertise grew and we performed at higher levels. As our department grew, we added staff and multiple trained individuals, which was also important for knowledge retention. With-

147

out good documentation and training, organizations cannot maintain a consistent standard of performance or grow their expertise.

This is one reason some small organizations stay small. Everything is known by a few people, and the organization can't grow beyond what they personally oversee. Documentation allows an organization to develop and learn from best practices, continue to improve, and efficiently train and engage others in the process so the organization grows. Documentation and training help make franchise models so successful.

When documentation and training are done properly, new hires don't start from scratch. They begin with documented knowledge of the previous job holders and often are able to add their unique perspectives and experience to improve the results. It's much quicker and more efficient to bring people up to speed with good documents.

Chapter 23

Progress Through Enabling Control Systems

How much more could you relax if you had an easy way to know things in your organization were under control?

If you had a system to keep things on track, how much time and energy would you save?

A great challenge many entrepreneurs face is empowering others and letting go appropriately. They do not know how to empower yet keep control. The behavior I see ranges from micromanaging with a "thumb in every pie" to giving instructions and never following up on the end result.

Enabling control systems

Most people don't like to think about control systems. They like them fine for other people but not for themselves. If the purpose of a control system is to oppress and stress people, then I don't like it either. But the real purpose of a control system should be to measure, provide meaningful feedback, and promote a sense of accomplishment and celebration. It helps the individual and the team stay on track.

- **What is control?** It's staying on track.

- **What does a control system entail?** A budget or target/goal, measurement of an initiative's status, comparison with the target, and corrective action, if necessary, to hit the target.

- **What does an enabling control system do?** It flags variance from the target. Ideally, that happens proactively through a system that gives early warning indicators. It indicates areas where correction is needed.

- **What is the value of measures in a control system?** If you don't choose the right items to measure, you might inadvertently ignore the organization's guiding principles or goals. Jack Welch, former CEO of GE, says if you can't measure it, you can't manage it. Choosing a very few balanced measures is key if a control system is to add value to the organization.

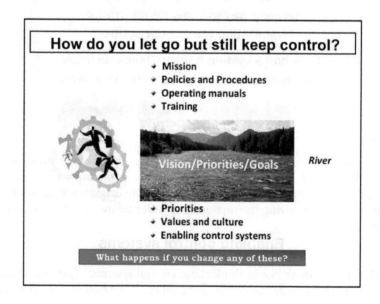

How do you let go but still keep control?

- Mission
- Policies and Procedures
- Operating manuals
- Training

Vision/Priorities/Goals   *River*

- Priorities
- Values and culture
- Enabling control systems

What happens if you change any of these?

Why should control systems be created? To enable individuals to accomplish the mission and vision of the organization. When control systems are formulated properly, leadership will know the status of all things that impact the organization's vitality. Some people and certain personality types like control just for the sake of exercising control. After years as an auditor, I believe firmly that control systems should never be about control for the sake of control. Nor should they limit an individual's freedom unless doing so protects people and is in the best interest of the organization.

Let's talk about how to set boundaries. Whom do you engage in setting the boundaries, and what is your attitude and motive? This brings us back to the "People" section of the book, where we looked at personality profiles.

- The "D" personality likes to feel in control but doesn't like getting into details and will tend to delegate the establishment of policies and procedures, operating manuals, and controls.

- The "I" personality doesn't like getting into the details either and tends to feel controls are abusive.

- The "S" personality is good at developing operating manuals and knowing how things are done and will appropriately engage in the development of manuals, policies and procedures, and controls.

- The "C" personality will tend to be more detail-oriented and risk-averse, and will design very tight controls. In many larger organizations, the "C" personality will volunteer to create boundaries.

The problem is, when you don't have all four personality profiles involved, you will tend to get boundaries too narrow and the organization's flow will be restricted. Then people comply but are not creative and proactive, or they rebel, work around the system, and you have less control.

It is a given that you can over-control and hinder progress. We have already discussed that. However, good and well-balanced control systems help detect problems early, before they get too big. They help keep us on track toward meaningful progress. What should a control system look like? From my experience, the simpler, the better. HCA had operating indicator reports that showed the standard, actual, and variance. Varying degrees of follow-up were initiated based on the degree of variance and its impact.

Quarterly Reviews

This is part of a good, enabling control system. In Lee Iacocca's book, he describes his turnaround efforts at Chrysler, including quarterly reviews or accountability sessions with each of his vice presidents. I adopted this practice with good results. Using this method properly, it's impossible to go more than 90 days with your direct reports being off-track toward their annual goals without your knowing it. Of course, I had more frequent contact and follow-up, but these quarterly reviews were comprehensive in nature. At the end of the year, my direct reports had already experienced three reviews with me regarding their progress. Therefore, the annual review was easy to accomplish, and there were no surprises. Quarterly performance reviews helped me in several ways. They:

- **Reduced my urge to micromanage** because I knew at the end of the quarter, I would receive a comprehensive update on the business and the performance of each of my direct reports.

- **Reduced my urge to get emotional and judgmental** instead of looking at objective performance data to which we had agreed before the year started.

- **Helped me stay on top of things.** One of the first things I did at the end of every year was to schedule quarterly reviews of all of my direct reports for the next year. I made it one of the highest priorities each year. We did three quarterly reviews for the year plus an annual review. This scratched my control itch because it ensured none of my team could be out of sync with our goals more than 90 days without my knowing about it and having an appropriate discussion.

- **Helped me coach the team appropriately.** Generally, people don't like quarterly reviews, or annual reviews for that matter. In training sessions when I talk about reviews, people in supervisory positions almost shudder. When I inquire, they all say it's a negative experience they dread. Their dread stems from a perception quarterly reviews entail talking to the person about what they're doing wrong. Supervisors see that as offensive to the employee and potentially conflict-oriented. Yet Millennials are especially open to coaching. They desire leadership and have reaped the core values of the BoXer generation.

  Kids grow up playing sports of various types led by coaches. Good coaches are always remembered and loved by kids for spending time with them and teaching them the game. Coaching in organizational life should be no different. It should be a growth and teaching opportunity that is constructive all the way around. Granted, coaching sessions will not be pleasant 100 percent of the time. But if you are hiring correctly and staying on top of change, pleasant coaching sessions should be the norm.

- **Helped me give positive feedback in a timely manner and create opportunities for celebration.** I am hardwired to be a management-by-exception person. But that's not most conducive for developing people and impacting morale positively. I don't want to go more than 90 days without talking to someone about their performance, thanking them for it, and bragging on them for something they've accomplished. I had good people, and 90-plus percent of the time, I would look forward to talking with them at their annual review. Several of my direct reports lived in different states, so I didn't get to see them regularly. When I did, I was genuinely happy to see them and excited about the opportunity to give them positive feedback. When coaching was appropriate, I wasn't shy about it because I really wanted to help them.

  If correction or discipline was needed, I would do it quickly in an effort for it not to be an issue at the end of the year, impacting their annual performance review.

  Wayne Carpenter, mentioned earlier in this book, gave me a valuable piece of feedback after he ran my personality profile. He told me we had a very healthy environment at HCA Physician Services. The people tended to work hard and be serious about their jobs. There was not a culture of fear. The people tended to enjoy their work and associates. Then he told me I went from one goal to the next without taking time to enjoy and celebrate success. As soon as he said it, I knew he was exactly right. So I used quarterly reviews and other forums to recognize people and celebrate accomplishment of individual or team goals.

Quarterly reviews are a great way to empower people with the goals to which they agreed and which they want to achieve but, at the same time, ensure you are staying on track throughout the year. There's nothing worse than getting to the end of the year, realizing people have missed their targets, and then trying to have a discussion about it.

Quarterly Review Format

The format of a quarterly review report is important, especially when someone is using the long form. For every bullet point in the standard column, there should be a corresponding bullet point in the year-to-date actual column. The same is also true for an end-of-the-year report. The proper way to complete the form is illustrated on the next page.

Quarterly Reporting

Quarterly performance reports should have three headings, the goal, the standards which determine success of the goal and the year to date status.

Sometimes there are multiple standards for a goal. In this case each one should be separated by a bullet point. For each bullet point in the standard column there should be a status bullet in the year to date column. They should be labeled as follows:

MET. "This means the goal has been fully met."

On track. " This means you are on track to meet the goal by the end of the year. In this case it's good to indicate a percentage completion.

Off track. "This means you're not where are you expected to be at this point in time. In these cases you should indicate if you will be able to get the goal back on track and when. If you will not be able to meet the goal by year end you should indicate why and what level of accomplishment you expect to Achieve.

NA. "This means not applicable as you did not expect achieve anything on this goal at this point in time"

See the following sample report:

Manager Goals Annual Report

Goal	Standard	Bonus	YTD Actual
1. Reduce overhead by redesigning staffing model	• Develop new model of 1 RN and 2 MA per team (reducing # of RNs) by 12/31/17	14%	• Met. Reduced RN by 6% and increased MA by 8%.
2. Use new phone system to develop call center	• Incoming calls addressed in real time 70% of the time. • All calls received by 3pm addressed same day • All calls received after 3pm addressed by noon the following day	15%	• Met • Not Met. Currently they are addressed by noon the following day. • Met
3. Finalize and implement incentive program based on productivity	• Develop matrix goal productivity based on # calls and patients seen by each nurse by 4/15/17 • Partners approve 4/30/17 • Pay bonus for 1st quarter based on productivity 5/1/17	14%	• Not Met. Due to staffing needs, we have abandoned incentive plan at this time as _____ is our only office manning majority of calls.

When the form is filled out correctly, it's easy to review in two to five minutes and know exactly where performance for this employee stands. I first look at the goals that are met or exceeded and brag on them for their accomplishment. We discuss any goals that are off-track. I ask questions to determine if it's because the goal was set too high, if the timing is off, if we will be able to catch up and meet the goal by year end, or if the person is shooting for a different target and why. This gives me a chance to coach the employee if appropriate or to ask for a corrective action plan if that is the best course of action.

My norm was always to show appreciation for achievement, ask questions that would let me understand better, and then reiterate my appreciation for what they had accomplished. I looked forward to the reviews and discussions. Most of my employees looked forward to them too.

See the example below of an annual report. When goals are set properly and the report follows the guidelines, it is easy to determine the results for an individual. It is the perfect catalyst for praise and recognition.

Sample Long Form Ministry Goals

	Goal	Standard	Year to Date
1.	Resource partners in the area of stewardship to advance our work.	• Achieve 7.5% giving average by December 2019 • Raise $1 million through special offerings by 12/31/18	
2.	Create online training for partners and other ministry leaders.	• One hundred leaders will have completed 100 hours on online training by 12/31/19 • Formal and informal surveys validate that at least 75% of participants believe the training will make a meaningful difference in their ministry and they will be able to give examples of such. • At least 50% of participants will show a desire for additional training and would recommend a friend receive some of the training.	

Chapter 24

Progress Through Measurement

> How much easier would your work be and how much more in control would you feel if you had a few measurable indicators telling you what you needed to know?

We like to keep score. Keeping score gives us a sense of accomplishment. Would you keep watching sports if scores weren't kept? Of course not. We have an innate need to create and be productive. Keeping score lets us know how we're doing. Measuring and reporting the right things can have substantial impact on the progress of an organization. Measuring the wrong things can hurt an organization. It impacts people positively if measurements are communicated and appropriate follow–up is initiated. So what do you measure? The simple answer is you measure the high priorities—those things that "move the needle." If you choose the wrong things to measure, then the enabling control system is of no value.

How do we keep score in organizations? An organization has measures it tracks daily, weekly, monthly, and annually. It knows exactly where it stands against expectations for those timeframes. How about the employees? Do they know how they're doing within defined time intervals? If you don't keep score and provide feedback, they are likely to experience some anxiety or insecurity that is not necessary if they are doing well.

You may say, "We can't measure everything we want the employee to accomplish." That is particularly true in certain complex leadership roles. You can, however, give feedback on high-priority objectives, as well as your perspective on performance relative to expectations.

What should we try to measure?

What to measure is tied directly to the mission, values, vision, and priorities of the organization. Special focus should be placed on priorities that have been agreed upon for the next year. When establishing measures, keep in mind what really "moves the needle." Having a few key measures narrows your focus to what contributes most toward your vision. Think about how a river works. The narrower the banks, the faster the water flows.

General Measures

In general, organizations tend to measure four things:

- **Cost** – What is the price?
- **Quality** – How good is it?
- **Volume** – How much do I get for the price I pay?
- **Time** – How long will it take to get it?

Generally, there are tradeoffs in these measures. When you emphasize one, you impact the others. If you want a higher quality product, you may have to pay more and it might take you longer to get it, though this is not always the case.

158

One mistake leaders make is not having balanced measures. If we measure quantity but not quality, we tend to produce poor quality goods or services. If we only measure quality but not quantity, we tend to be less productive. If we focus only on cost and trying to reduce it, we may negatively impact quality.

I've seen numerous examples of new initiatives in organizations where measures were not kept in balance. One company did a massive computer conversion where the information technology department was incentivized based on the number of conversions, but not the quality or the downstream costs of a poor conversion. The results were predictable.

In Physician Services, as we rolled out new service lines, we had to balance the speed of the rollout with maintaining the quality of the program. There were times when hospital or division operators wanted something done very quickly. Responding to those requests and doing things more quickly than we knew was prudent always caused problems we had to fix. In the end, acting too quickly took longer than doing it right in the first place. Often, our leadership in Physician Services found themselves working hard to put the brakes on programs so we could implement them at a speed that would not create additional problems.

Detailed Measures

In the *Four Disciplines of Execution*, Chris McChesney, Sean Covey, and Jim Huling distinguish between two types of measures.[10] Lag measures are the traditional result-oriented measures to which most people are accustomed. They occur weekly, monthly, quarterly, and annually. In other words, these are simple measures of what results we achieved. Lead measures are more activity- and behavior-oriented. Lead measures are:

- **Predictive**
- **Influenceable**
- **Impactful**

Lead measures track activities that can predict and influence a result. An example could be losing weight.

The goal: lose 50 pounds in one year

- **Lag measure**: The number of pounds I actually lost at each the end of each reporting period.
- **Lead measures**:
  - Drink 80 ounces of water daily
  - Walk 60 minutes daily
  - Eat five small meals daily of 300 calories each

Leveraging Measurements

I saw HCA leverage measurements in the area of accounts receivable. As a company, the days of accounts receivable were just too high. On average for the company, invoices were outstanding some 70 to 80 days before payments were collected. Leadership thought 55 was a reasonable standard. So what did they do? Simply announce that 55 was the standard? What would that change? They did introduce some promotion and fanfare. They printed stickers and created banners that said, "Stay alive at 55." But things began to change when leaders published results and comparisons of the operating units. Now that there was a contest, about 10 percent of the business office managers in the company wanted to have the lowest days of accounts receivable. So they started working on ways to improve the results. And they improved. After 18 months, the top business office managers had their days of accounts receivable average less than 40.

What about the others? Well, some of the business office managers began to learn from those who had better results. Their days in accounts receivable went down as well. In some divisions, training programs were implemented, and several of the business office managers improved their results. In some cases, business office managers were not able to learn enough from others or the training programs to improve the results. Some looked for easier jobs, and others were asked to leave.

Here was the dynamic I observed. When the worst days in receivable for a division were 90, the office manager at 80 or 85 was comfortable. When the worst came down to their level, they got really busy looking for ways to improve. The end result after 18 months was that the worst hospital was at 55 days, and the company average was about 47.

Let's make application to organizational life. Who sets the performance standard? Most operating managers say management does. I ask, "How?" They say, "We set the performance goals and standards." I ask, "Are they always met?" Rarely does anyone say yes. So I ask again, "Then who is setting the standard?" The real answer is the "weakest link in the chain," the people known to have the lowest level of performance and who continue to keep their jobs in the organization. As long as everyone else can look at those people and know they're doing better, they feel safe. And that is fine as long as those people's levels of performance are acceptable.

The bottom line is this–to get improvement, do these things:

- Measure and publish results

- Create a contest where the top performers can compete

- Create opportunities for the lowest performers to learn from others

- Offer training to help people meet the performance standards

- Make a change in personnel if people are not qualified for the job

All these tactics have their place in an organization. They produce tangible results when used correctly.

> **What you measure impacts what people give their attention to.**
>
> **How you report results drives people's reaction to measurements.**

When used properly, measurements can encourage and motivate teams and individuals in healthy competition and learning activities. I do not suggest using them to manipulate people.

Progress Section Questions

1. Does your team set and own their goals?

2. What kind of mistakes do you make that could be avoided?

3. Do you set clear, measurable, and objective goals?

4. Is your documentation good enough that you can lose key staff or lay leaders and still carry on?

5. Are the things you measure really meaningful?

6. Do you do quarterly reviews with your team?

Chapter 25

From Bricklayers
to Cathedral Builders

How much better would your results be if you
could change people from bricklayers to
cathedral builders in your organization?

We defined cathedral builders, builders, and bricklayers at the very beginning of this book. I think everyone would agree that healthier, more
vibrant organizations comprise cathedral builders. These are people
who have the:

- Personality profile for their jobs
- Preparation to contribute at high levels
- Potential to grow
- Passion to commit to projects because the vision excites them
- Connection to projects through a sense of their life's mission or
  calling

163

It makes so much sense, yet we see organization after organization, including churches, ministries, and nonprofits, staffed with a combination of bricklayers, builders, and cathedral builders. So what are the keys to building a team of cathedral builders? Of course, this whole book is about that. Let's look at it this way: What aspects of organizations and leadership styles tend to create bricklayers rather than cathedral builders?

Lack of missional focus

Staying focused on a clear mission is valuable for the organization in multiple ways. It helps fight against mission creep, which inevitably happens to most organizations unless they have an intentional focus on their mission. Mission creep creates confusion for team members and dilutes their enthusiasm.

When the organization has a worthwhile mission, people take pride in being part of it. They feel important because they are part of something bigger than themselves. Without that, people just tend to do the work and look for feelings of worth and contentment in other areas of life.

Unclear or uncompelling vision

The vision needs to be clear and repeated often. Vision creates a picture of a better future and a sense of optimism among the team. The vision needs to be compelling to each team member so they have passion about being part of it. If they don't see how they connect personally to the vision and their part in accomplishing it, then it is not a motivator.

Lack of vision leads to despair. Despair leads to going through the motions and yields disgruntled bricklayers. Where there is no vision, the people perish.

Unclear or changing priorities

Priorities need to be clear and consistent. Constantly changing priorities move people from being cathedral builders to being bricklayers. Without a clear goal in mind, people do not know how to take initiative and use their creative talents. When priorities change frequently, employees doing the work see the waste in changing directions. They get worn out and start to simply do what they're told. Plus, they have no sense of excitement or satisfaction from their work.

Wrong people

Everyone was created to be a cathedral builder. People may be bricklayers or builders only in your organization under your leadership. What inhibits people from being cathedral builders in your organization? You may have:

- Hired the wrong personality profile. They are not working out of their core strengths and might be like a fish swimming upstream or carpenters cutting a board against its grain. In most organizations I consult with, only two-thirds of top executives have the right personality profiles for the roles in which they serve. Think about how much worse the percentage may be when you go down the organizational hierarchy.

- Hired someone without the appropriate level of skill and training. In this case, they can only do what they are told because they don't know enough to be proactive.

Unempowered people

Even if you have the right people, you must empower them to capture all they want to and are able to contribute to the organization. If you are looking over their shoulders and micromanaging them, it will cause them to think and act more like bricklayers than cathedral builders. You will not get initiative or creativity unless people are fully empowered.

Failure to measure and share success

You have to measure to know how well you're doing. It's critical that success and progress be shared with the team. How many people would even watch a sporting event if they didn't keep score to know who's winning? People need to win. They need to know the organization is making progress, and they need to understand that they are contributing to it. Measuring and sharing progress gives the organization information to coach individuals when needed. This is positive in itself. But most importantly, measuring progress provides the basis to celebrate progress. Without the celebration of teams and individuals, people feel unappreciated and unfulfilled because they don't know how much they are contributing to the team or if the team is winning. They are more like bricklayers than cathedral builders.

Failure of leaders to own the result

The Navy SEALs have an interesting approach to leadership training. In their book *Extreme Ownership*, former SEALs Jocko Willink and Leif Babin describe a process where nine teams are formed.[11] The teams execute various drills, many of which they do with heavy rubber boats on their shoulders. The best team gets to rest and the worst team has to do additional work. This gives the best team a natural advantage the next time they have to perform and the worst team a natural disadvantage in the next set of drills.

After several drills, they move the leader from the worst team to the best team. They also take the leader from the best team and place him in charge of the worst team. What do you think the results are? Some improvement by team number nine and some decrease in performance by team number one?

Actually, in the instance described by Willink and Babin, the very first drill after the change saw the former team nine become the best performing team. I would have expected some improvement, but not anywhere near that dramatic. What do you think the difference was? The best team leader coordinated, encouraged, and challenged the team. He got them to work cohesively as a team. The worst leader cursed, blamed, and criticized his team. They got frustrated and didn't work well as a team.

The next big surprise was that the team with the worst leader did not fall to the bottom. They actually became team two. The point here is that when an organization or team of people is used to functioning correctly, they can continue good habits even when there is a change to bad leadership.

166

An entire book was written on this topic. I highlighted it here to make this simple point. Leadership really does matter. The difference between an organization of bricklayers and an organization of cathedral builders lies in its leadership.

**The difference between an organization of bricklayers
and an organization of cathedral builders
lies in its leadership.**

APPENDIX

Personality Profile Application

Work

God gifted people with all kinds of talents to express in doing His work. Maybe you've heard the age-old question, "Are leaders made or born?" Do you know who asked that question? Academicians! The same people don't ask if artists were made or born or if musicians were made or born. It's rather obvious they have a special talent or gift that is developed and refined through much practice. The same is true with leaders. They are born with a special gift or talent that they work hard to develop and refine. Can someone who is not a natural artist be trained to draw? Yes, but they will only be proficient to a certain degree. Can someone sing or play a musical instrument without being gifted musically? Yes, but there will be a limit to what they can do. The same goes for leaders. People can be trained in certain skill sets, but they can never be as effective as a naturally gifted leader.

In the work environment, people can be trained to do a great variety of things. The key is to find what they're naturally gifted at and let them refine and perfect their natural talents. Far less success ensues when people are assigned tasks that take a great deal of effort but at which they will never be great. One thing to look for in hiring people or giving them assignments is what they are naturally good at. What do they feel they were created to do? The hardwiring, or personality profile, of an individual will give us some help in knowing what he or she is naturally good at.

- The "D" personality likes to initiate ideas and come up with new projects. They like to take charge or control the project.
- The "I" personality likes to sell or promote the idea. They're concerned about the people aspect of the project. They like to handle the social part of the project.
- The "S" personality likes doing things. They enjoy doing the work. They want to do whatever it takes to make the team successful.
- The "C" personality likes to improve upon the idea. They are very technical and analytical. They are able to make most things work better.

The following chart illustrates the work each personality enjoys most.

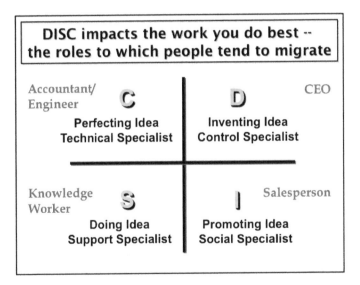

Failure to understand personality profiles can create problems in planning projects. The "D" personality, who came up with the idea, wants to control it and does a lot of talking. "D" types tend to tell other people what to do. The "I" personality wants to be supportive. He or she starts promoting the idea and also does a lot of talking. The "S" personality, who's going to do a lot of the work, wants to be accommodating and goes along with the idea. The "C" personality tends to see flaws in the plan. But unless these types feel strongly about it or are specifically called upon, they will not speak up. They fear being ridiculed or criticized for not going along with the team. Therefore, plans are made quickly and promoted without the solid input of people who know how to execute the plan or how to improve upon it. When plans get off-track, stress is introduced into the equation and the dynamics get worse.

Reactions Under Stress

Dynamics change when stress is introduced into the equation. The chart below shows how people respond under stress.

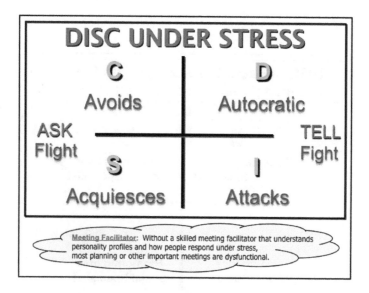

- Under stress, the "D" personality becomes very autocratic. They start telling everyone what to do. The "I" personality begins to attack. This is counterintuitive. The person who has been the cheerleader and social specialist starts attacking people. This is one of the most surprising changes in behavior I see when stress is introduced. Both the "D" and "I" personalities are prepared to fight when stressed.

- The "S" personality wants to make peace. They will give up their position to make others happy. Their stance is, "I'll do whatever you want me to do. Can't we just all get along?" The "C" personality tends to be quiet and reflective. Unless they feel strongly about a matter or are called upon, they may not speak up. Also, they will get very upset if they feel any criticism for a failure is being directed toward them.

- These dynamics illustrate how organizational life can become messy. Stress is usually introduced when something has gone wrong. The personalities doing the talking, the "D" and "I," don't know how to do the work or improve on the work but are giving the directions. The personalities with the most insight in how to get the project back on track, the "S" and "C," are acquiescing or avoiding the discussion altogether.

- In such a situation, a good leader needs to recognize the personality profile of each team member and the strengths each brings to the table. The leader needs to draw the "S" and "C" personalities into the discussion to get their expert perspectives. Then, the "D" personality needs to chart a course, and the "I" personality needs to sell the new approach.

HCA went through a major merger in the 1990s. In my department, the teams of three former companies were being merged. I volunteered to handle the planning process to integrate the three former departments into one. All four major personality types were represented on the leadership teams of the three former departments. As you would expect, the person in the room with the highest "D" personality, besides myself, wanted to talk first and often. Next to speak were the ones that had the highest "I" components. As the facilitator, I let them talk. After an appropriate time, I asked that we listen to other team members. I called on the "S" personalities first. They knew most about how to get the work done. Next, I called on the "C" personalities. They tended to be most shy and generally would not talk unless asked their opinion in group settings. Yet they would identify potential problems no one else saw, ask deeper questions, and improve upon a good idea.

171

After hearing from the "S" and "C" personalities, I asked the "D" personalities for their perspective on executing and controlling the project. I asked the "I" personalities for input on how this would impact people and be received.

When we combined all these perspectives, we had a much better plan that engaged the entire team with their unique perspectives. Fewer problems and adjustments were necessary later than if we had used a different approach.

The DISC Profile and How it Works

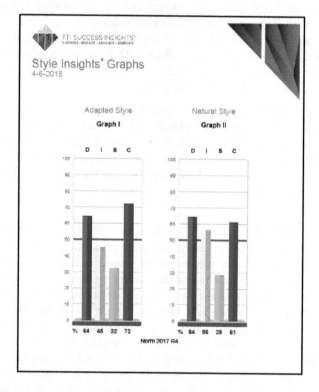

The graphic above contains sample results from a DISC personality profile. The red bar represents the "D" personality which, as you recall, is the driver. The yellow bar represents the "I," which is the influencer or life of the party. The "S" bar represents the steady, process-oriented personality, and the "C" bar represents the cautious, compliant, and analytical personality.

There are two graphs on the page. One is labeled natural style. This is the inner self with which you are most comfortable. It's what your graph would look like if you worked for yourself, most likely. It's also what you revert to under extreme pressure. In other words, it represents your core. The other graph is labeled adapted style. It is how you think you are supposed to act in the environment where you currently operate. Typically, this reflects your work style.

It's also helpful to look at a person's work style pattern illustrated on the next chart. In hiring, it is critical to determine the needed style pattern before you begin recruiting.

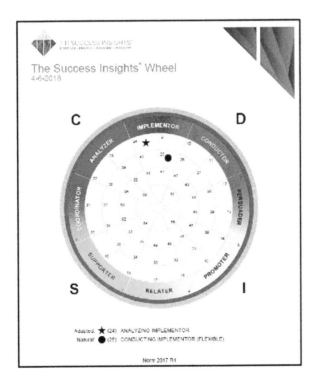

This diagram shows the individual's overall style. It plots natural and adapted styles on a wheel. The first thing you should do before the hiring process begins is determine the pattern you're looking for, or at least the acceptable range of patterns. If you don't know this, you may hire a person with a good résumé and that you like a lot but who is really not best qualified for the job. I could probably write a whole book with examples of how this works.

In one instance, I was coaching a group of doctors. They were very high-producing, busy doctors. Therefore, there was a lot of nursing turnover. I worked with the clinical director to do some back testing to determine the profiles of the nurses who had the most success with these doctors. They tended to be in the coordinator/supporter range. If they got too close to the analyzer range, they tended to be very accurate but too slow to document notes and process patients. If they were too close to the relater pattern, patients tended to really like them, but they chitchatted so much with people that they didn't get their work done fast enough.

How Should You Use Personality Profiles In Hiring?

I. Identify styles, patterns, or acceptable range of ideal candidates on TTI profile

II. Review resumes for potential candidates

III. Screen for acceptable profile

IV. Compare TTI profile to resume and AI profile for consistency and to validate accuracy of each

Look for weaknesses in profiles that would prohibit the person from being successful in the role

V. Use what you learned from profiles to strengthen interviews

---

In preparing to do an interview, determining the style pattern and acceptable range relative to the position is key.

ENDNOTES Part 1

Note #	Reference	Text Page
1	Viktor E. Frankl, *The Meaning of Life*	Page 1
2	Module 7: *Organizational Direction, Vision, Mission, Goals, Objectives,* McMonkey-McBean, page 2. Available from http://quizlet.com/11265967/module-7-organizational-direction-vision-mission-goals-objectives-flash-cards	Page 17

ENDNOTES Part 2

3	Dr. Henry Cloud, *Necessary Endings*	Page 37

ENDNOTES Part 3

4	Google.com, Positional Power definition, page 1. Available from https://www.google.com/#q=positional+power+definition	Page 46

ENDNOTES Part 4

5   Dan Miller, *No More Dreaded Mondays*
     (New York: Random House, 2009).   Page 65

6   Kent J. Wessinger, PhD, Research at
     create2elevate.com   Page 79

7   Kent J. Wessinger, PhD, Research at
     create2elevate.com   Page 80

ENDNOTES Part 5

8   Blog.gaiam.com, Quotes by Robert Greenleaf,
     page 1. Available from http://blog.gaiam.com/
     quotes/authors/robert-greenleaf   Page 86

ENDNOTES Part 6

9   Dick Wells, *16 Stones* (Franklin, TN: New
     Vantage Publishing Partners, 2012).   Page 139

10   Chris McChesney, Sean Covey, Jim Huling,
     Four Disciplines of Execution   Page 159

11   Navy SEALs book, *Extreme Ownership*   Page 166

Image Credits

Diana Rush – Organizational charts and DISC graphics

Clip art and photos are taken from Microsoft Word stock images.

Front and Back Covers – Darrell Girardier © Copyright 2020 Vision Leadership Foundation

178

Take a healthy view of the people you lead . . .

. . . AND THE PAIN YOU AVOID MAY BE YOUR OWN. Whether people are a boon or a bother really depends on you. On whether you help them feel like they count. On whether you make it clear where you're leading. And on whether you convince them that going there is what they want, too. You can be a great steward of an organization's resources only if your're a blessing to people. So assimilate the leadership know-how in this book, and establish the right perspective on the people you employ. Because the success of your company, organization, division, or department depends on *you*.

Do you feel like you're working harder than ever?

BUT NOT GETTING ANYWHERE personally or professionally? If so, author Leon Drennan can help. In The Power of Purpose and Priorities, he explains how to reassess your mission, values, and purpose in order to gain focus in your activities and develop priorities. Drennan says "less is more" when it comes to scheduling in business, family life, and social engagements. Wise people learn to prune away all nonessential activities in their personal lives and organizations to optimize the use of resources.. "You have to be clear about your purpose before you can set meaningful priorities for how you spend your time in this life," Drennan writes. "But more importantly, you have to be clear about your purpose and committed to it to have the endurance to see your priorities through. When you combine a clear understanding of your purpose with a few focused priorities, your life will have much greater impact."

When God created humans . . .

. . . HE HARDWIRED THEM TO MAKE PROGRESS in life and even commanded them to do so. Millenia later, the need for progress remains acute especially for those in leadership roles. In *Empowering Progress*, Leon Drennan charts a path to fulfilling this basic human drive for men and women in leadership. The key, he says, is to know the steps necessary to achieve progress and then empower people in an organization to take those steps effectively. For real progress to occur, the process must be guided by a servant leader who understands the nature of power and uses it to serve others. Only then will an organization be empowered to progress.